Archaeology Data Service

Geophysical Data in Archaeology:
A Guide to Good Practice
Second Edition

By Armin Schmidt

With contributions from Tony Austin,
Andrew David, Kate Fernie, William Kilbride,
Paul Linford, Julian Richards and Damian Robinson

Produced by Oxbow Books on behalf of the Arts and Humanities Data Service

ISBN 1 900188 71 6
ISSN 1463 - 5194

A CIP record of this book is available from the British library

This book is available direct from

Oxbow Books, Park End Place, Oxford OX1 1HN
(Phone: 01865-241249; Fax: 01865-794449)

and

The David Brown Book Company
PO Box 511, Oakville, CT 06779, USA
(Phone: 860-945-9329; Fax: 860-945-9468)

or from our website
www.oxbowbooks.com

Printed in Great Britain by
The Information Press, Eynsham, Oxford

Contents

Acknowledgements

The working party that authored this *Guide to Good Practice* would like to offer sincere thanks to those who have contributed to it by reviewing and commenting on draft versions. These people include:

Arnold Aspinall, University of Bradford
Fred Bettes
Adrian Brown, English Heritage Centre for Archaeology
Paul Cheetham, Bournemouth University
Rinita Dalan, Southern Illinois University at Edwardsville
Peter Hinton, Institute of Field Archaeologists
Chris Gaffney, GSB Prospection
John Gater, GSB Prospection
Mike Heyworth, Council for British Archaeology
Bill McCann, The Clark Laboratory, Museum of London Archaeology Service
Mark Noel, GeoQuest Associates
Joep Orbons, RAAP Amsterdam
Julian Richards, Archaeology Data Service
Mike Tite, Research Laboratory for Archaeology and the History of Art, University of Oxford
Roger Walker, Geoscan Research
Alistair Webb, West Yorkshire Archaeology Service
Mark Whittingham, West Yorkshire Archaeology Service

This Guide was edited by:
Kate Fernie, Archaeology Data Service
Maureen Poulton, Archaeology Data Service
Damian Robinson, Archaeology Data Service
Armin Schmidt, University of Bradford

The authors and editors of this Guide would also like to extend their thanks to all those who have worked so hard to bring it to publication. These people include:
Jo Clarke, Archaeology Data Service
Val Kinsler, 100% Proof

Section 1: Introduction

1.1 AIMS AND OBJECTIVES

This *Guide to Good Practice* is concerned with the variety of data that may be produced during geophysical survey projects and how to ensure that they can be preserved in digital formats for future re-use. The digital preservation of geophysical data is important. Effective digital archiving ensures that the data generated during a survey are available for reprocessing and re-interpretation in the future. The single most important consideration for long-term digital archiving is the accurate documentation of data, their collection and subsequent management procedures. This is necessary to ensure that people re-using the data understand both how they were created and why. It is not only the raw geophysical data measured with instruments in the field that are of concern; processed data and interpretative drawings are equally important, as is the written survey report.

The results from *Strategies for Digital Data*, a recent survey by the Archaeology Data Service of digital data in archaeology (Condron *et al.* 1999, 29-32), show that a wide variety of organisations are both creating and holding digital data for excavation and fieldwork projects. For this reason the *Guide to Good Practice* is aimed at:

- Creators of digital archives, including contracting and consultancy units, university-based research projects and national and local societies.
- Agencies and bodies commissioning archaeological fieldwork, including national heritage agencies and local authorities.
- Curators who will receive excavation and fieldwork digital archives, including museums, National Monuments Records and county or regional Sites and Monuments Records.

1.2 DIGITAL PRESERVATION OF GEOPHYSICAL DATA

Throughout this *Guide to Good Practice* the importance of digital preservation is stressed. The discipline of archaeology is in a special position, as much data creation results in the destruction of primary evidence and consequently organisations need to take their archiving responsibilities very seriously. While non-invasive survey techniques like geophysics do not destroy primary evidence, the preservation of the information created is no less important. Preservation is necessary in order to maintain a complete record of past research, to prevent unnecessary duplication and to allow the re-use and re-interpretation of the collected data as analytical techniques evolve.

All geophysical survey data are digital and they may be the only record of a site investigation. Preserving this information in digital formats requires special care and attention since, with the ever-increasing pace of change in computer hardware and software, that data may become irretrievably lost within a few years.

Digital preservation is different from traditional archiving. Archives usually preserve physical objects (e.g. paper, photographs, microfilm). Digital archiving is about preserving information regardless of how that information is stored. This is because disks and other magnetic media degrade and software and hardware change rapidly: the physical media on which digital data are stored are not permanent. The content, structure and context of the information, however, *must* be preserved. Consequently, the best strategy for the long-term preservation of archaeological data is to collect them systematically and then maintain and make them accessible to users operating in very different computing environments. The data must be migrated from one medium and format to the next through changing technology so that their intellectual content remains available in the future.

Digital archiving strategies do not, and should not, rely on the preservation of a single disk, tape, or CD-ROM. The essence of digital archiving lies in short-term security measures (e.g. secure back-up, data refreshment, and data storage) coupled with long-term preservation strategies (e.g. migration) and thorough documentation (see Section 4).

1.3 HOW BEST TO USE THIS GUIDE

Ideally, any individual or institution involved with, or planning, a geophysical survey with the long-term aim of depositing the resultant data with the ADS should read this *Guide* in its entirety. However, in many cases individuals or institutions are involved in different stages of the overall process. To reflect this the *Guide* has been structured into clear thematic sections, and documentation pathways relevant to specific tasks are suggested.

1.3.1 Pathways through the *Guide to Good Practice*

The following sub-section contains some suggested documentation pathways. These relate to tasks undertaken by different individuals or organisations involved either in planning or carrying out geophysical surveys. In each case, a practitioner is identified and the relevant sections of the *Guide* are highlighted. The pathways presented are not intended to be exhaustive nor to be viewed as a prescriptive list. Tasks frequently overlap and it is often the case that individuals involved in undertaking the geophysical survey are also intimately involved in project planning and archiving.

Practitioners are encouraged to use the pathways presented here as templates to develop their own 'good practice' check-lists.

Specifying a brief
- Reasons for a survey project (sub-section 2.3)
- Planning for the creation of digital data (sub-section 4.2)
- Guidelines for depositing a digital archive (sub-section 6.1)
- Acceptable deposit formats (sub-section 6.2.1)
- Report (sub-section 3.9)

Tendering a project design

- Choice of survey methods and procedures (sub-section 2.4)
- Contacting a digital archive (sub-section 6.1)
- Determining the required metadata and documentation (sub-section 5.2)
- Report (sub-section 3.9)

Planning a survey

- Planning for the creation of digital data (sub-section 4.2)
- Secure backing-up (sub-section 4.3.1)
- Project documentation (sub-section 3.2)
- Documenting the geophysical survey (sub-section 3.4)
- Data treatment (sub-section 3.5)
- Survey methodology (sub-section 3.5.1)

Planning to deposit an archive

- Description of archive (sub-section 3.10)
- Determining the required metadata and documentation (sub-section 5.2)
- Guidelines for depositing a digital archive (sub-section 6.1)
- Acceptable deposit formats (sub-section 6.2.1)

1.3.2 The thematic sections

In order to cover all types of geophysical data this *Guide* is structured around the various stages of a project and highlights important considerations related to data at each stage.

Section 2 introduces the possible reasons for conducting a geophysical survey project. It considers how these reasons impact upon the data, and how they can best be documented in the digital archive.

Section 3 takes up the issues relating to the documentation and management of data at each stage in the life-cycle of a project. These stages may be defined as:

- initial desktop research,
- in-field documentation – the establishment and location of grids and raw data collection,
- data analysis and interpretation, and
- dissemination phases – including the creation of a report and a fully documented archive.

Section 4 offers guidance on digital preservation of archaeological geophysical data and general issues related to digital archiving.

Section 5 examines which parts of the project documentation discussed in Section 3 are required as 'metadata' to find and retrieve resources from an archive for a particular purpose.

Section 6 concludes with notes on how to deposit archaeological geophysical data with the Archaeology Data Service and the English Heritage Geophysical Survey Database.

The *Guide* is not intended to provide information on how best to undertake archaeological geophysical surveys; it neither prescribes procedures nor can it guarantee optimum results. The methods employed during a project's fieldwork and analytical phases, however, can affect the feasibility of the long-term digital preservation and consequently some discussion of field practice is necessary. For detailed information on how to conduct archaeological geophysical fieldwork it is recommended that readers consult other sources (Clark 1996; English Heritage 1995; Gaffney *et al.* 1991; Scollar *et al.* 1990).

1.4 OTHER SOURCES OF INFORMATION

1.4.1 Other archives of geophysical survey information

The English Heritage Geophysical Survey Database (EH GSdb online: http://www.eng-h.gov.uk/ SDB) provides an index of all geophysical surveys of archaeological sites carried out by the Centre for Archaeology (formerly the Ancient Monuments Laboratory) of English Heritage, and also includes surveys by others. The database is intended to be a first point of reference for those interested in ascertaining which sites have been surveyed by English Heritage since 1970. The database holds details of each survey including the site location, the techniques used, the sampling intervals, the client, along with a summary of results and a listing of relevant publications. Survey reports prepared since 1993 are available in full online. English Heritage aims to expand this useful resource by including the results submitted by teams conducting surveys over Scheduled Ancient Monuments and by inviting information from others acquiring similar data.

1.4.2 Other Guides to Good Practice

This *Guide to Good Practice* is one of a family of six theme-specific guides, commissioned by

Service Provider	Title of *Guide*
Archaeology Data Service	Geophysical data in archaeology: a guide to good practice
	Archiving aerial photography and remote sensing data: a guide to good practice
	Archaeological databases: a guide to good practice
	CAD guide to good practice
	Digital archives from excavation and fieldwork: a guide to good practice
	GIS guide to good practice

Table 1: Archaeology Data Service Guides to Good Practice

the Archaeology Data Service. Taken together the *Guides* comprise a comprehensive, authoritative and highly complementary set of practical guidelines.

It is important to recognise that this *Guide* provides information concerning how to prepare and deposit digital material in an archive. Although it provides some recommendations regarding the facilities and procedures for the creation and maintenance of a digital archive, these are covered more fully in the Arts and Humanities Data Service's *Managing Digital Collections* series of publications that is available online (http://ahds.ac.uk/managing.htm). Equally, this *Guide to Good Practice* is written to address archaeological practice in the United Kingdom, although (where possible) it makes recommendations that are applicable internationally.

The ADS is part of the Arts and Humanities Data Service which caters for digital archiving needs across the humanities disciplines of archaeology, history, literary studies, performing and visual arts. Each AHDS Service Provider takes responsibility for advising on good practice in the creation, management, preservation, and re-use of digital information widely used in its subject area, and each is publishing their own *Guides to Good Practice*. A number of guides are currently planned across the AHDS (Table 2).

Service Provider	Title of *Guide*
History Data Service	Digitising history: a guide to creating electronic resources from historical documents
	Secondary analysis in historical research
	History GIS
Oxford Text Archive	Creating and documenting electronic texts
	Finding and using electronic texts
	Developing linguistic corpora
Performing Arts Data Service	Data creation in performing arts
Visual Arts Data Service	Creating digital information for the visual arts: standards and best practice
	Using digital information in teaching and learning in art and design
	Why invest in the digitisation of visual arts material

Table 2: Other Guides to Good Practice from the Arts and Humanities Data Service

The most up-to-date information on the other *Guides* in the AHDS series is available online (http://ahds.ac.uk/guides.htm).

Section 2: Archaeological Geophysics

2.1 INTRODUCTION

Archaeological geophysics is the application of ground-based geophysical methods to help elucidate the location and character of buried archaeological features.

The geophysical techniques commonly applied in field archaeology may be categorised as either active or passive:

- *Active techniques* are based on the injection of signals into the ground (e.g. an electric current or electromagnetic wave) and measurement of the response at the ground's surface.
- *Passive techniques* rely on physical attributes that would exist even in the absence of a measuring device (such as the magnetic field of a buried kiln).

Whatever the physical parameter being measured, the usual result of a geophysical survey is a matrix of data points, or transects of data, across a site. Following some data processing, patterns generated in these data can be interpreted in terms of buried archaeological features. The results are generally presented as either a two-dimensional site plan (e.g. in a conventional area earth resistance survey), or as a diagram showing the data from a transect as a section across the site (e.g. Ground Penetrating Radar (GPR) profiles). Multiple transect images can be compiled into a three-dimensional data set which can be visualised as two-dimensional images at increasing depths. These are called *depth slices* and for GPR data are derived from *time slices*.

The interpretation of geophysical surveys can be augmented by the inclusion of geoarchaeological and geochemical information, sources which can also provide archaeological insights in their own right. The former includes the use of augering and test-pitting, while the latter includes measurements of trace elements or phosphates. As geochemical data can be closely associated with geophysical surveys, and the methodologies of data acquisition and display are often parallel, the guidelines to follow can mostly also be applied to these types of data.

2.2 HISTORY OF ARCHAEOLOGICAL GEOPHYSICS

Most geophysical techniques used today for archaeological investigations were initially developed for geological or civil engineering applications. While the underlying physical principles are the same, the shallow depth and relatively small size of archaeological features test the laws of geophysics to limits that are not often encountered by 'conventional' geophysicists. Research into these particular problems led to the development of a sub-discipline now called 'archaeological geophysics'.

Clark (1996, 11) describes how in 1893 Lieutenant-General Augustus Pitt-Rivers hammered on the ground with a pick to identify a ditch from the variation of the sound – the first recorded application of a geophysical technique for archaeological prospecting. After 1945 the great potential of aerial photography was increasingly exploited. However, the available photographs often lacked positional accuracy which was then only achievable using ground-based techniques. In 1946 Richard Atkinson successfully started earth resistance surveying and the technique was subsequently boosted by the development of transistorised equipment (the Martin-Clark earth resistance bridge in 1956, and the Bradphys automatic earth resistance meter in the late 1960s). The adoption and theoretical study of new electrode arrangements, particularly suitable for buried archaeological features and fast area coverage (Aspinall and Lynam 1968), and the automatic logging of data (Kelly *et al.* 1984) again boosted the use of this technique. While improvements are still ongoing (see for example the development of vehicles with electrodes fitted to their wheels (Panissod *et al.* 1998) or the advances in vertical resistivity pseudosections (Aspinall and Crummett 1997)), earth resistance surveying has established itself as one of the key methods for geophysical prospecting in archaeology.

The development of another successful technique, magnetometer surveying, was started in 1958 by Martin Aitken with the use of a proton magnetometer. Interest in the technique was spurred by the discovery that not only fired kilns and ferrous objects would show magnetic anomalies but also soil features such as ditches and pits. Irwin Scollar used the differential sensor configuration for large-scale surveys from 1963, and in 1966 began with automatic digital recording on punched paper tape. Also in the 1960s, fluxgate magnetometers, which allowed continuous recording due to improved measurement speed, were introduced by John Alldred and Frank Philpot. Limitations of sensitivity then led to the deployment of Alkaline vapour magnetometers (sensitivities of 0.01nT) by Beth Ralph, Helmut Becker and Peter Melichar in the 1970s. These instruments have since been perfected and high-resolution surveys of large areas are now feasible (Eder-Hinterleitner *et al.* 1996).

Active electromagnetic methods are increasingly used for the investigation of archaeological features. Most notably, Ground Penetrating Radar (GPR) is now a well-established tool that combines high sensitivity and spatial resolution. Initially greeted enthusiastically (Stove and Addyman 1989), it was deployed under unsuitable conditions (wet clay soils) and acquired a bad reputation amongst archaeologists in Britain. With better understanding of the technique and its limitations, this perception has been redressed and GPR is now used successfully on many sites (Conyers and Goodman 1997).

Geophysical data capture is now entirely digital, and the increasing size and sampling resolution of modern surveys is resulting in the accumulation of vast quantities of data. An example of large-scale geophysical surveying is the Wroxeter Hinterland Project (online: http://www.bufau.bham.ac.uk/newsite/projects/WH/Tours/geophysics.html) which has involved several survey teams, using a variety of methodologies. The magnetometer survey alone, of some 78 hectares, recorded nearly three million data points.

2.3 REASONS FOR A SURVEY PROJECT

Before beginning a geophysical project, it is important to consider carefully the data that are required as these will structure the fieldwork. Hence it is useful to examine the reasons for undertaking the project so that appropriate survey methodologies can be planned. Reasons for undertaking geophysical surveys usually fall into four broad categories, although these are far from mutually exclusive:

Field evaluation in advance of development – Geophysical techniques are used increasingly, in conjunction with other means of field evaluation, to provide information on the presence and character of archaeological remains on sites for which development is proposed. Since such remains must be identified prior to receipt of planning permission, and should in principle be preserved wherever possible, methods of non-destructive evaluation are now deployed with increasing frequency. There are many different types of development pressures, but geophysical methods have found particular application on sites of mineral extraction, commercial and domestic buildings, road and rail routes, pipelines and other infrastructural links. In some cases, results from such investigations have led to further archaeological research.

Site management – Geophysical techniques are also used to help locate and characterise archaeological remains which are not covered by planning legislation: agricultural ploughing and coastal erosion are two examples. Geophysical techniques can also aid the identification and characterisation of sites of national importance where active management, including legislative protection, may be necessary. The information provided by surveys can significantly increase knowledge of sites and improve their interpretation and presentation to the public. Work within and around World Heritage Sites such as Stonehenge provides one example.

Archaeological research – Whether or not there is a planning or management incentive, geophysical methods are often used directly in support of specific archaeological research. Research objectives can include the detailed study of individual sites (e.g. Sutton Hoo), or can be widened to address categories of monument type (e.g. Wessex hillforts), wider research themes (e.g. early iron-working), or landscape-based studies.

Technical research – Surveys are also undertaken in order to research the geophysical techniques themselves, often in situations where there is an additional archaeological advantage. Whilst the routine methods of magnetometer and earth resistance surveys account for much of the development-led work and archaeological research referred to above, there remains a need both to refine these methods and to introduce new ones. Research is currently aimed, for instance, at increasing the sensitivity and resolution of detection and exploring methods of three-dimensional data interpretation.

2.4 CHOICE OF SURVEY METHOD AND PROCEDURE

Advice on the choice of survey methods and procedures is available in published guidelines and scholarly literature (Clark 1996; English Heritage 1995; Gaffney *et al.* 1991; Scollar *et al.* 1990). Advice may also be obtained directly either from the Centre for Archaeology (formerly

Ancient Monuments Laboratory) of English Heritage, or from other professional geophysicists or geophysical consultants. The adequate training and qualification of personnel undertaking surveying and interpretation is essential.

A geophysical survey, if not a finite project in its own right, is more typically a component of a wider project and usually conducted at an early stage in the life of that project. It is thus important to ensure that specialist advice is sought at an early stage and that any survey is carefully scheduled within the project timetable.

The choice of survey method(s) will depend on several variables, the relative balance of which will vary from site to site. The most important of these are:

- the survey objectives
- archaeological questions
- previous aerial photographic evidence
- previous geophysical survey results
- current land use
- previous land use
- underlying solid and drift geology
- other local geomorphological and topographic factors
- degree of access to land
- time, money and personnel available for the survey

Most of this information can be gathered and assessed by desk-top consultation, although preliminary site reconnaissance and/or a pilot survey may also be appropriate. Once these factors have been assessed, an appropriate methodology can be designed utilising the optimum combination of techniques and sampling strategy for the site in question (English Heritage 1995).

Records of the planning stages of a geophysical survey project form a vital part of the project's digital archive, and it is therefore essential to document any initial research undertaken and decisions made. Such documentation is generally included in the project report (see Section 3.9) and produced in a standard word-processed text that will evolve into the core of the project's digital archive.

Section 3: Documenting Data from a Geophysical Survey Project

3.1 INTRODUCTION

When archaeologists think of 'documentation' they generally think of the reports presenting information about a project's history, archaeological background and results. Such reports are a vital component of a complete archive. However, to enable the re-use of digital data produced by geophysical surveys, a more specialised form of technical documentation is additionally required, which should record which file formats are in the archive, which software applications were used to create them and so on. When taken together, such documentation enables the effective description of the resource; an essential prerequisite for its re-use. It is therefore recommended that the following documentation should be supplied, where appropriate, for any geophysical survey archive:

- Project background, methodology and results
- Description of the survey's coordinate system
- Digital data documentation
  - survey documentation (e.g. size of grids, traverse spacing, instruments used)
  - data storage (e.g. format of data, how do the files fit together, software used to create them)
  - data analysis (e.g. filters applied to the data, images with interpretation drawings)

This is no more than would be expected as part of good professional practice for all archaeological geophysical projects. However, the potential re-use of digital data makes it particularly important that this information is clearly reported. Consequently, this section sets out project documentation, georeferencing the geophysics coordinate system, and documenting survey techniques. It then discusses data storage, treatment, interpretation and imaging.

It is recognised that much of this information will be routinely incorporated into the publication of a survey report. Extracting this information from a report, however, is often cumbersome and time consuming. It is therefore useful if the information can also be provided in a tabular format, especially since parts of it are often already stored in project databases. Although the preparation of a fully documented archive is introduced in this section, its purpose is to recommend *what* should be documented, not *how* it should be reported.

It is useful to view each geophysical survey as an individual 'event' – a geophysical investigation over a specific area within a particular period of time. Under this model, surveys carried out at the same location but at different times would usually be recorded as separate events. However, if several surveys were undertaken under very similar conditions (e.g. weather, land use) and especially with the same grid system, they may be taken together as one survey event; this should be clearly indicated under the item *Duration* (see section 3.2).

3.2 PROJECT DOCUMENTATION

Documentation is important. Although in any geophysical survey project the data measured by the instruments will be logged either automatically or manually, additional information that could influence the interpretation of the data may not be formally recorded. This may include information about local geology or the weather conditions on the day of the survey, how the instrument was set up, how the survey was orientated, and where the survey grids were located. While seemingly obvious at the time of the survey, it is essential to archive this information for future use by the survey team and others.

The types of information recommended for inclusion in the project documentation for any geophysical survey event are listed below. This documentation does not necessarily have to be provided as a list or table but may simply be included in the survey report (although its recovery from such text may be cumbersome). It is the information itself which is important, not the format in which it is recorded.

Survey name
: The name of the site, project or survey. It may either be the name used in a written report (e.g. 'A46 Widening Scheme: Area B') or the familiar and/or published place or monument name where this exists (e.g. 'Stonehenge, Lesser Cursus').

Survey index
: The identification number/code used internally for the survey event and the related data.

Survey purpose
: A brief summary (max. 200–300 words) of the main aims and objectives of the project from which the data collection arose and the purpose of the geophysical survey (see Section 2.3). [A summary of the survey's *findings* can be recorded under the heading *Report Summary* (see Section 3.9)].

Bibliographic references
: Relevant bibliographic information about the site or project.

Survey keywords
: Keywords indexing the subject content of the data set. They can be drawn from the data fields listed below (e.g. Solid/Drift geology, Monument type, Period, Survey type etc.) with reference to appropriate documentation standards (see Appendix 3) or if a local documentation standard is used this should be included with the data set.

Spatial coverage
: The map coordinates of the SW and NE corner of a bounding box enclosing the survey area. British National Grid coordinates are recommended and should be given at least to the nearest 100m 'six figure grid reference'. It should be noted that such map coordinates

may be inaccurate (up to several metres), and also that the Ordnance Survey of Great Britain (OS) holds copyright over the reproduction of OS maps and retains Intellectual Property Rights in all information derived from such maps. In addition, there may be instances, for example, at sites where there is a threat of looting, where locational information must remain confidential (especially if access to the geophysical data might lead to criminal activity). In such cases it may be necessary to restrict or omit locational information (including clues from which a location can be deduced) from publicly accessible records.

Administrative area   The District/County/Unitary Authority in which the survey area lies. The administrative boundaries that are current at the time of the survey should be used and, for consistency, the use of the standard names from Appendix 3 is recommended.

Country   The country in which the survey was undertaken (England, Northern Ireland, Scotland, and Wales should be indicated separately).

Solid geology   The underlying solid geology, recorded using current British Geological Survey terminology. Any extra information from other quoted sources may be useful. In some cases a site may cover a number of different geologies, in which case they should all be listed. See Appendix 3 for a list of possible terms.

Drift geology   Relevant drift geology for the survey area. As with *Solid Geology* the site may cover a number of different drift geologies that should all be listed. See Appendix 3 for a list of possible terms.

Duration   The dates of the first and last day on which the fieldwork took place. If separate periods of fieldwork are related to the same survey event (see above) they should be listed individually.

Weather   A brief description of weather during fieldwork, with clear additional reference to previous conditions (e.g. 'dry and hot after a prolonged period of heavy rain').

Soil condition   A brief description of the soil conditions during fieldwork (e.g. very dry, dry, moist, wet, water-logged, frozen).

Land use   The land use at the time of the survey. The term used should be drawn from the list given in Appendix 3.

Monument type   A classification of any archaeological monument known to exist at the site or that was revealed during the survey. Use of the *Thesaurus of Monument Types* (RCHME 1995) is recommended to achieve consistency in terminology (see Appendix 3); any uncertainty can be indicated by a '?'. In many cases, a survey will cover several monuments from different periods and all relevant types should be

	listed. The text of the accompanying report should describe how this interpretation has been derived: from existing archives, publications or as an interpretation of the collected geophysical data.
Monument period	The periods of any archaeological monuments on the site. Use of the period terms listed in the *Manual of Data Standards for Monument Inventories* (MIDAS) is recommended (RCHME 1998), see Appendix 3.
Scheduled Ancient Monument (SAM) number	Any sites within the survey area which have been included on the Schedule of Ancient Monuments should be identified by their county SAM number. This information is included on the relevant survey licence (e.g. issued by English Heritage) or can be obtained from the Sites and Monuments Record (SMR) held by the Local Authority.
Surveyor	The name and address of the organisation or individual(s) who carried out the geophysical survey.
Client	The name and address of the organisation or individual(s) who commissioned the survey. Such information may be confidential and may be withheld in some cases.
Depositor	The name, address and role of the organisation or individual(s) depositing data related to the geophysical survey.
Primary archive	The name and address of the organisation or individual(s) holding the primary data from the survey.
Related archives	References to the original material for any data derived in whole or in part from published or unpublished sources, whether printed or machine-readable. Details should be given of where the sources are held and how they are identified there (e.g. by accession number). If a digital collection is derived from other sources it should be indicated whether the data represent a complete or partial transcription/copy, and the methodology used for its computerisation. Also full references to any publications about or based upon the data collection should be provided.
Copyright	A description of any known copyrights held on the source material.

3.3 DOCUMENTING THE GEOPHYSICS COORDINATE SYSTEM

Accurate positional information is important if geophysical data are to be combined with other spatial data sets or used to locate buried archaeological features. There are many different ways to establish a geophysics coordinate system – for example compass, tapes, Total Station,

GPS. The choice will depend on the site, available instrumentation and intended use of the geophysical data. This section will explain how the location of the geophysics grid can be documented and what information is required to assess the spatial accuracy of any interpretations that are derived from it.

The concepts underpinning geospatial references are discussed in more detail in Appendix 1. It is important to remember here that geophysical data are normally recorded in a homogeneous rectangular coordinate system, indexed by line and point counts, or 'Eastings' and 'Northings'. This mathematical reference frame is in reality warped over an undulating surface so that it has to be stretched in all directions to fit.

There are two possible approaches to finding the 'real' position of a geophysical anomaly on the ground. Either the geophysics coordinate system is physically re-established on the ground or the geophysics grid is mapped to another coordinate system (e.g. a site grid defined with a Total Station, the National Grid, GPS coordinates), which can more easily be used on site. The former approach requires a very careful documentation of the procedure for setting out the geophysics coordinates ('georeferencing'). The second approach calls for detailed information on the mapping between the different coordinates ('reference frames', see Appendix 1.2), often referred to as 'coregistration'. In any case, to assess the certainty with which the position of geophysical anomalies on the ground can be identified (e.g. in order to locate an excavation trench), information is required about the accuracy of the procedure for setting out the coordinate system or its coregistration.

In addition, it must be remembered that geophysical data are not 'images' of the subsurface but have spatial characteristics that need to be considered when inferring the location of causative buried features (Clark 1996; Scollar *et al.* 1990). For example, magnetometer anomalies recorded in the northern hemisphere show a positive peak to the South and a negative trough to the North of the underlying feature.

The laying out of grids and setting out a site are well established techniques and covered in detail elsewhere (e.g. Bettess 1992). This section describes how to *document* this procedure. In a second part it discusses how to record coregistration information.

3.3.1 The geophysics coordinate system on the ground

The geophysics coordinate system is often laid out on the ground (e.g. using tapes or optical squares) and a network of characteristic points is established (e.g. corners of grid squares of 20m x 20m). Once created it can be recorded so as to provide coregistration information (see 3.3.2 below). However, it is also useful to document the procedure for establishing this network so that it can be recreated if necessary (e.g. if the instruments for recording the coregistration information are unavailable, or if exactly the same system is required to do further geophysical surveys).

In many cases the geophysics coordinate system is set out from a 'baseline', a line placed across the site as a reference for all other measurements. It can normally be assumed that spatial accuracy decreases further away from the baseline and it is useful to lay it roughly through the middle of the site. Often secondary baselines are placed at right angles to subdivide larger fields. The desired network of markers (e.g. at corners of grid squares of 20m x 20m) can then be filled in with other methods (e.g. using tapes). Finally, a fine mesh (e.g. 1m x 1m) may be established to provide easy reference for each recorded geophysical data point. While these are the typical steps for the creation of a geophysics reference network on the ground, each survey team will use a slightly different approach. It is therefore important to document all steps carefully so that the final result can be replicated.

To locate the coordinate network on the site some characteristic points (e.g. the ends of a baseline) should be identified by reference to 'reasonably permanent' ground features (e.g. the concrete base of a pylon). The following georeferencing information is required for each referenced point:

- detailed description of ground features used for reference (e.g. 'bottom of SE corner of base of pylon'),
- tape measurements to at least two such ground features,
- estimated accuracy for relocating the reference point when using above information. This may take into account, for example, errors due to the possible stretching of a tape, wind blowing tapes about etc.

To describe a baseline one can either:

- provide georeferencing information for two of its points (e.g. start and end points, see above)
- provide georeferencing information for one point (e.g. its start point) and a compass bearing. The latter should be accompanied by an estimate of the error (e.g. '± one degree') and the date of the recording since magnetic north changes slightly with time.

If the site is further subdivided into a network of markers it is useful to describe briefly how this was achieved, e.g. 'secondary baselines set up with optical square; pegs inserted for 20m x 20m grids using tapes of 20m and 28.28m'.

It is important to provide an estimate of the accuracy with which the markers can be re-established using this method. For example, if it was found during the set-out procedure that corners of grid squares were about 0.1m out from their intended position when measured from different points along a baseline, this information may be used; or if the method for finding a right angle contains an error of approximately ± one degree the resulting spatial error at the end of a secondary baseline can be derived.

3.3.2 Coregistration to other coordinates

To use a different coordinate system (e.g. a site grid defined with a Total Station, the National Grid, GPS coordinates) for the geospatial referencing of geophysical data, the coregistration between the geophysics coordinate system and the other coordinates needs to be defined. In most cases the mapping between the two 'reference frames' will be based on control points identified in both systems with their respective coordinates (see Appendix 1.3).

Site grid

Sometimes, a site grid has already been set out with pegs, for example for an excavation or for field walking. If the geophysics coordinate system coincides with this site grid no further transformation between the different coordinates is necessary. Often, the two systems will match at a number of individual control points (e.g. the corners of 20m x 20m grids) but in between the correlation can be poor. It is important to provide clear indications as to which control points were chosen for the overlay of the two grids. While the re-use of an existing site grid can be convenient, it should be remembered that it may have been set out with a different requirement for accuracy (e.g. coarse for field walking) or information on its definition may not be easy to obtain. It is therefore useful to record independent georeferencing (see above) and coregistration information (see below).

Instrument-defined grid

'Instrument-defined site grids' are characterised through the instruments used for their set-up. For example, Total Stations and GPS rely on an implicit model of space; the Total Station uses a flat horizontal projection and the GPS uses the WGS84 datum (see Appendix 1.5). These instruments can be used to locate control points within their respective coordinate systems very accurately (sub-centimetre accuracy is possible). For these points both the coordinates of the geophysics system (e.g. grid corners, points along the baseline established according to the procedures discussed in 3.3.1) and of the instrument's site grid will be recorded. They can then be used to define the coregistration. The accuracy of all measurements in both coordinate systems should be documented carefully. A Total Station should be related to clearly identified ground features so that its implicit site grid can be recreated. With GPS-derived information it is also necessary to record information on its set-up (e.g. position of a base station).

While mapping between the two coordinate systems may be accurate at the control points, there can be considerable discrepancies in between. The number of control points used will determine the overall accuracy of the mapping. Sites with pronounced changes in topography require more control points to reduce such errors. It is stated in Appendix 1.3 that a minimum of two control points may be sufficient on a totally flat surface. However, at least four points (e.g. the corners of the survey area) should be used on more varied terrain and recording additional control points is highly recommended. For coregistration, some software tools do not map the two coordinate systems exactly at the control points. Instead a smooth transformation with the smallest possible errors (e.g. least squares polynomial transformations) is calculated. This may result in additional spatial inaccuracies and should be considered when evaluating the coregistered data later.

Maps

Where a map of a site is available (e.g. from a national mapping agency like the Ordnance Survey of Great Britain or from an earthwork survey) it is useful to relate other coordinate systems to the information in the map. For this, control points should be chosen which can be easily identified on the map. Coregistration can either be directly to the geophysics coordinate system or, in an intermediate step, to the site grid. In any case, the chosen control points should be clearly described to allow their identification on the map.

Frequently, discrepancies arise between measurements (distances and angles) made on the map and on the ground. To assess which measurement is correct the accuracy of the information used needs to be known (e.g. several metres for a map and 0.01m for a Total Station site grid).

It is recommended that the following information is recorded for coregistration:

- brief description of the site grid (e.g. references used for setting up a Total Station),
- a list of control points. If coregistration with a map is planned at least some should be chosen to be well-defined map features and described clearly,

- the coordinates of the control points, both in the geophysics coordinate system and the site grid,
- information on the accuracy for these coordinates.

3.4 DOCUMENTING THE GEOPHYSICAL SURVEY

Some information about the survey techniques used during a survey is required. This will help to assess the suitability of the archived geophysical results for later re-use. Such information would enable questions such as, for example, 'was the sampling interval close enough to detect narrow and shallow ditches?'.

The following is a list of the forms of documentation that might be useful to record for each survey technique on each individual survey event:

Survey type

The category of geophysical technique used should always be recorded. The following list, while not exhaustive, gives examples of survey types:
- magnetometer
- magnetic susceptibility – including volume or mass specific
- earth resistance surveys
- vertical resistivity section – including pseudosection or tomography
- electrostatic
- low frequency electromagnetic – including conductance, susceptibility, in-phase, quadrature
- GPR
- seismic
- microgravity
- magnetotelluric
- VLF
- radioactivity

Instrumentation

Specific information about the type and configuration of the geophysical instruments used (e.g. specific probes or antennas) is required to assess the information available. As an example, it could be recorded that a 'Geoscan FM36 Fluxgate Gradiometer' or a 'SIR2 GPR system from GSSI with a 400 MHz dipole antenna' was used for a particular survey event.

Area surveyed

It is helpful to have an indication of the area of ground covered with each survey technique, as this allows a quick estimate of the quantity of data collected. The unit of measurement used should be clearly stated (m^2 or hectares are equally acceptable).

Method of coverage

To assess the extent of the survey coverage it is important to record the method by which the ground was covered and the data were acquired. Possible methods are:

- regular grid (i.e. the recording positions are at regular intervals in two directions)
- single traverses
- spot samples (i.e. the recording takes place at arbitrary positions)
- scanning

Traverse separation   The separation (or distance) between adjacent lines should be recorded in metres where a series of parallel traverses (a 'regular grid') is used to collect data for a particular technique. The size of detectable features may be assessed using this information together with the *Reading interval*. Such information should be documented explicitly even if it is stored with the measured data (see Section 3.5, *Resolution*).

Reading interval   If data are recorded at regular intervals along the traverses, the distance in metres between adjacent readings should be noted.

Sampling position   The exact position where data were recorded, whether within the grid squares or at grid corners (e.g. '0.5m in both directions from the SW grid corner').

Grid size   If data were collected over individual grids their size (or dimensions) should be documented for ease of data coordination (e.g. '20m x 20m').

Accuracies   The accuracy of recording, both in terms of the spatial accuracy (i.e. how well the measuring position matches the recorded position) and of the recorded values (i.e. the level of signal noise). If this is too difficult to quantify, it may suffice to document the recording mode in detail, for example whether automatic or manual triggers were employed, which data range was selected on the instrument, and whether data were collected while moving or stationary

Additional remarks   It is important to note any other technical aspects of the survey which may have a bearing, such as instrumentation problems, or the use of non-standard techniques.

3.4.1 Additional documentation for earth resistance, magnetometer and ground penetrating radar surveys

In addition to the above, the following additional documentation is required for earth resistance, magnetometer and ground penetrating radar surveys.

Earth resistance surveys

Probe configuration   The earth resistance response from shallow features depends strongly on the electrode configuration used. It is therefore important to record this information for a thorough interpretation of the results. Examples of possible probe configurations include:

- twin-probe
- Wenner
- equidistant double dipole ('Wenner-beta')
- general double dipole
- Schlumberger

Probe spacing

The depth to which features are recorded depends on the electrode separation used, so it is extremely important to record the distance between adjacent electrodes, for example on a mobile twin-probe frame.

Magnetometer surveys

Magnetic North

The orientation of the geophysics coordinate system relative to Magnetic North is important for the interpretation and processing of magnetometer data and an accurate record should be made. The use of a compass is recommended, as Magnetic North differs from True North and varies slightly with time.

Instrument drift

The instrument used for the geophysical survey may show a gradual change of its readings with time ('drift'). If information on such drift is recorded regularly (e.g. after the completion of each grid for an FM36 fluxgate gradiometer) the effect may be compensated by the use of appropriate software. Details of the method used for monitoring the instrument drift and the measured drift itself should be documented (e.g. 'log zero-drift after each grid at common position').

Ground penetrating radar surveys

Timing

In order to interpret the results from a GPR survey and to associate the plots with a vertical scale, it is important that information on the time delay for the recording of the first reflection, the time sampling resolution and the maximum time span of the recording are noted. This will allow an assessment as to whether the data provided are investigating deep or shallow ground and what size of features may be detectable.

Dielectric permittivity

If possible, an estimate should be made of the averaged ground permittivity in order to allow a preliminary conversion between delay times and depth, although only sophisticated processing ('migration') can deliver a true depth scale. Providing estimates of the velocity of electromagnetic waves in the ground is equally acceptable.

3.5 DATA STORAGE

Before examining possible formats for the storage of geophysical survey data and associated documentation, it is important to consider the desired use of that data as this will determine the level of documentation necessary. For this, three broad levels of processing can be defined:

- **Data improvement** – Some common surveying errors can be rectified with appropriate software if information on the process of data acquisition is available. For example, if it is known that data were collected on adjacent lines, drift in the instrument's background signal can be eliminated. However, processing can only be applied if data are available in a format that reflects the surveying procedure (e.g. if data are saved as separate grids) and the survey methodology is documented.

- **Data processing** – Where the full range of measurement values is available, processing algorithms can be applied that relate to the geophysical nature of the acquired data (e.g. effective highpass filtering, or reduction-to-the-pole for magnetometer data). In this case, all collected data can be assembled into a large 'composite' before further processing is carried out.

- **Image processing** – When data are converted into images for display purposes, accurate spatial information is often lost and the full range of data values is compressed to the limited resolution of a palette (e.g. 256 shades of grey) that suits a particular display best. These images can then only be treated with standard image processing tools, which cannot take into account the full range and geophysical nature of the underlying data.

To allow basic *Data improvement*, most software used for geophysical data manipulation stores measurements in a format that reflects the surveying procedure. Some information on the method of data acquisition is automatically recorded with the measurement data. For example, data are often stored in individual grids and information on the grid size, traverse spacing etc. are recorded as well. Therefore, all related computer files have to be kept together to archive this information.

The format of these files is often specific to the software used but in many cases can form the base for an appropriate archive (see Section 6.2 on formats accepted by ADS). However, it should be remembered that the software package may become obsolete or different versions may produce incompatible data. Therefore it is necessary to specify which software was used to create the data and in what version.

To cater for future generations of computers and to allow users of other software packages access to the data, it is useful to provide technical information on the layout of the files (e.g. '4 byte floating point binary'), and to specify any special values which have been reserved to indicate missing data ('dummy values'; e.g. '2047.5' or 'NUL') or over-range readings of the instrument. Such information is often included with the software's documentation or may be obtained from the software manufacturer.

3.5.1 Survey methodology

In addition to archiving these files, the survey methodology should be described briefly to help assemble the data at a later time. The following should be documented for each survey technique:

Grid layout	If data were collected over individual grids it is important to know where they are located in the geophysics coordinate system to assemble them into an overall layout. There are two possible approaches to documentation: 1 If all grids are of the same size, their arrangement can be indicated in a table or spreadsheet using the appropriate file names. 2 For arbitrarily sized grids the coordinates for each grid's lower left-hand corner can be supplied with an indication of its size.
Grid size	The dimensions (in metres) of the grid along the x and y axes ('Eastings' and 'Northings') of the geophysics coordinate system. This is recommended (see section 3.4) as part of the general survey documentation, but should also be recorded separately for each grid if the grid size changes across the survey area.
Resolution	The spacing between measurement points in the x- and y- direction. This information corresponds to the above-mentioned items *Traverse separation* and *Reading interval* but it may be necessary to record it for each grid individually.
Survey direction	The direction in which the first traverse of the grid was surveyed and where the subsequent traverses are located. If, for example, surveying began in the 'top left' corner of the grid, walked from 'left' to 'right' and then on subsequent lines from 'top' to 'bottom', this could be described as 'survey direction in positive x-direction, subsequent lines added in negative y-direction'.
Line sequence	The way in which the grid was walked: in parallel lines always in the same direction, or back and forth (zigzag surveying). This information needs to be recorded if destriping or destaggering of data is to be carried out.
Drift value	If the instrument used is able to record the drift across a grid (e.g. an FM36), this value can facilitate drift correction and may be provided for each grid.
Bias value	Should data be logged with an offset value subtracted, it is important to record this information for each grid.

As stated above, most software packages save data and additional information in proprietary formats which are incompatible for use with other geophysics software. To alleviate the problem of software-dependent file formats, an open interchange format is being developed in collaboration with ADS (Archaeological Grid Format; Schmidt forthcoming) which will allow a comprehensive digital description of gridded geophysical data.

In most software packages it is possible to save and archive data in an 'xyz format'. They are stored as ASCII data in three columns; the first two represent the coordinates of a measurement position in the geophysics coordinate system and the third column holds the measured data value. One disadvantage is the large size of these files. It should be remembered that information on the survey methodology must be recorded in addition to these files (see 3.5.1 above).

3.6 DATA TREATMENT

After measurement, data are corrected for common surveying problems (see section 3.5); they are usually assembled into a single large 'composite' holding all data. This compilation discards information on the underlying survey procedure (hence the data can no longer be referred to as 'raw') but instead allows processing to improve the overall appearance (see below). Most software packages save composite data in a proprietary format and all associated information files have to be archived together. Documenting the software used and its version is important. Composite data can also be saved in 'xyz format' (see section 3.5.1). It has to be stressed that composite data should not be used as a primary archive of geophysical data since essential survey information is already lost. Only raw data (e.g. individual grids) with information on survey methodology (see Section 3.5 and 3.5.1) provide the information necessary for later re-use.

There are many data processing functions available to the archaeological geophysicist (see for example Clark 1996, 150, and Scollar *et al.* 1990, 488). It should be borne in mind that processing may remove the signature of archaeological features (e.g. linear features parallel to the survey direction may be lost when destriping the data) or introduce artefacts specific to the processing functions (e.g. the introduction of negative halos when applying highpass filters (Clark 1996, 151)). It is important to give as much detail about the processing 'history' of a data set for later interpretation. Fortunately, most specialised software packages allow inspection of the history of the processing steps. Such history, together with information on the computer program used and its version often proves helpful in assessing the alterations to the original data. If details of the processing functions are known, or uncommon software has been used, it is advisable to give more detailed descriptions of the processing or refer to relevant publications. The information on the processing can be provided in a tabular format suitable to the applied tasks or as a brief description in a report. It may be helpful to describe why the individual processing steps were performed and what improvements they brought about.

The format in which processed data are saved and archived is normally identical to the composite data discussed above.

3.6.1 Rectification

Rectification is a particular type of data processing. It involves spatially stretching (or 'rubber-sheeting') of a geophysical data set such that it is represented in another coordinate system. For example, using coregistration information (see 3.3.2) the geophysical data recorded over an undulating surface can be re-calculated and directly overlaid onto a flat horizontal site grid (see Appendix 1.2.3). Rectification techniques range from simple affine transformations to complex multi-point polynomial procedures, depending on the level of irregular stretching involved. In addition, a range of interpolation functions are used to calculate data values at new positions. If these details are recorded and the underlying coregistration information provided it will be possible to assess the spatial accuracy of the rectified data. This is often very important, since the aim of many geophysical surveys will be to locate features on the ground! If rectification is combined with other processing functions it is useful to note the order in which the steps were applied.

3.7 INTERPRETATION

It is common practice to provide simplified interpretation diagrams to present and describe the results of geophysical surveys. Often, these take the form of vector drawings produced with CAD or GIS software, in the same way as for other archaeological surveys. Further details on the production of CAD drawings and the different formats in which they can be archived are given in the ADS *Guide to Good Practice* on CAD (see Section 6.2 on formats accepted by the ADS).

To allow for a combined visualisation of interpretation drawings and geophysical data, they need to be available in a compatible coordinate system. Either the geophysical data have been coregistered (see Section 3.3.2) and rectified to a common coordinate system (e.g. a site grid), or interpretation diagrams use the original geophysics coordinate system. In any case it is imperative to indicate which coordinate system was used for the interpretation diagrams.

In many instances, it may be acceptable to use a simple computer drawing package (vector or raster) to produce interpretation diagrams. This may be sufficient to print the diagrams in the format required but it often does not allow the use of the drawings for any other purpose (e.g. as a layer in a GIS); they have simply become images.

3.8 IMAGES

Converting geophysical data or interpretation diagrams into images will enable their digital or print presentation. However, much of the underlying geophysical information becomes unavailable for further processing unless the original data is also archived separately (see Section 3.5). While the creation of images provides a valuable resource for an archive, the provision of related data on spatial information, the range of geophysical values and so on, should not be neglected.

The simplest possible image will just contain a visual representation of the geophysical data (in any of the known display modes; see Clark 1996, 132). As such it is very helpful to give an impression and preview of the results.

To allow the retrieval of at least some quantitative information, however, additional details must be included on an image. The following features are considered useful:

Scalebar or scale and geographic reference
To allow spatial measurements to be made from the images (for example if access to raw data is difficult) information on the spatial dimensions should be provided. This can be in the form of a scalebar or four pass marks (see below). The latter are advantageous as they specify dimensions in both directions. It may sometimes be sufficient to provide an explicit scale (e.g. '1:1000'), but it should

be borne in mind that the latter may be altered when printing or displaying on different media or when resizing the image.If North is indicated on the image, and a point or line included which is geographically referenced (e.g. with National Grid or site coordinates), it will be possible to interpret the image in its geographical context.

Coordinate lines or pass marks

An alternative to the use of scalebars and North arrows is the inclusion of a coordinate grid with the image, but it is important to specify which coordinates are used (e.g. geophysics coordinate system, site grid or National Grid). An alternative approach is to provide four pass marks around the image with their respective coordinates. This allows for some distortions.

Data legend

A legend is required to derive quantitative information from the geophysical data presented in an image (e.g. the range of values). For example, if using a greyscale or colour plot, a palette bar annotated with some characteristic data values can be included. The same is true for continuous pattern plots (e.g. dot density). If contour diagrams are used it is possible to annotate each contour, provide a legend for different line types or indicate the increment between contours.

It is important that each image is accompanied by a figure caption giving the usual details. Figure captions can be stored as separate text files in an appropriate format (see Section 6). For archiving it is recommended that the caption is saved for each image in a separate file with the same file name as the image (e.g. 'fig1.txt').

Section 6, Table 8, details the digital image formats that are accepted by the ADS. It should be remembered that some image formats (e.g. JPEG with normal compression options) result in loss of data contained within the original image and should be avoided as archival formats. The preferred archival format for images is in uncompressed TIFF files.

3.9 REPORT

Each geophysical survey project should result in a report which compiles the evidence and guides readers through the interpretation of data. Information on writing project reports is provided by the Institute of Field Archaeologists (online: http://www.archaeologists.net/ standards/) and English Heritage has also published detailed guidelines (English Heritage 1995, 30).

English Heritage recommends that, as a minimum, reports should contain:

- non-technical summary – (an abstract)
- introductory statements – (site location and description, survey objectives)
- methodology – (dates, survey location, geophysical instruments used, methods of data collection and data processing)

- results – (description of anomalies, interpretation)
- conclusion – (degree of achievement of objectives, summary of results, implications)
- references and acknowledgements
- supporting illustrations at appropriate scales
- supporting data, tabulated or in appendices – (e.g. georeferencing and coregistration)
- index to and location of archive and
- appendices (technical details of methods and processing)

3.9.1 Documenting the report

The report itself and some basic cataloguing information should be deposited as part of the archive from geophysical survey projects. The information required to document the report is:

Report title and reference number
The title of the initial paper or digital report that has been generated from the results of the survey, and any surveyor's reference number.

Report author
The author(s) of the report.

Report holder
The name and address of the organisation(s) or individual(s) from whom copies of the report, or data, may be requested. Often a copy of the report may be deposited with the relevant SMR. In some cases permission may be required from both client and surveyor to access the report.

Report summary
A brief description of the findings of the survey. In many cases this will be the abstract of the full survey report.

Table 8 in Section 6.2 gives details of the formats for text documents preferred by the ADS for digital archiving purposes.

3.10 DESCRIPTION OF ARCHIVE

Only the creator of a digital archive is normally familiar with its structure; for example which files belong together, what their names mean and which software was used for their creation. If this information is not carefully documented it will be difficult to preserve the resource for the future. For example, if no information is available on the software used to compile geophysical data into composites, it will be virtually impossible to migrate them to a current data format – one of the most complex tasks of digital archiving (see Section 4.4).

To request detailed information on each archived computer file is impractical as it imposes a substantial burden on the creator of a digital archive. However, a simple list of all files with more detailed descriptions of related files should be possible. The following information should be provided with a digital archive:

List of all file names
A list of all digital files in the archive, with their names and file extensions (e.g. 'grid1.dat', 'site.cmp'). Such a list can be created for example using the MSDOS command 'dir > list.txt'.

Explanation of codes used in file names	A brief explanation of which naming conventions and abbreviations were used for the labelling of the files (e.g. 'magnetometer grids start with an "m" and are then indexed with a subsequent number: m1, m2, ...' or 'grids were labelled with letters increasing towards East and numbers increasing towards North, then followed by an indication of the instrument used: A1_m, A1_r, B1_m, B1_r, ...').
Description of file formats	An explanation of which internal format is associated with a particular file extension (e.g. '.rep files are Contors report files').
List of codes used in files	A list of special values used in the data (e.g. '2047.5 indicates a "dummy" value in the data').
Hardware, software and operating systems	It is useful for future data migration to provide this information where possible.
Date of last modification	The date of last data modification allows the currency of the archive to be assessed.
Description of known errors in data	If errors are known to exist in the data (e.g. an instrument was malfunctioning for parts of the survey) they should be briefly indicated.
Indications of known areas of weakness in data	This information helps to assess the value of the data for future use.

3.11 CASE STUDY: THE COTTAM PROJECT

By Julian Richards

The presence of Anglian and Anglo-Scandinavian settlements at Cottam, East Yorkshire, was first indicated in 1987 by numerous finds by metal detector users of coins, dress pins, strap ends and other copper alloy artefacts. The Department of Archaeology, University of York, carried out a programme of fieldwork on the site between 1993–1995 which included fieldwalking, geophysical survey and excavation. The results of this fieldwork were published in the *Archaeological Journal* 156 (1999) and, by kind permission of the Royal Archaeological Institute, in *Internet Archaeology* 10 (2001). The digital archive has been deposited with the ADS, while the finds and paper archive from the project are deposited with Hull Museum.

The geophysical survey was carried out between October and December 1994. The aim of the survey was to produce a detailed map of sub-surface geophysical anomalies within two sites defined by concentrations of metal finds. The southern concentrations also coincided with a cropmark enclosure. The survey was also to act as a pilot study to assess the relative effectiveness of magnetic and earth resistance techniques in mapping anomalies in this area.

Two survey areas were located in the northern part of the large field to the west of Burrow House Farm. Area 1 (NGR 49760 46674) was situated over the central and eastern part of the concentration of cropmarks forming a large enclosure with several associated smaller enclosures.

Area 2 (NGR 49763 46690) was sited over two small sub-rectangular enclosures to the north-east of the larger cropmark site. Both areas were subsequently examined by excavation.

In the field the geophysical data were downloaded from the surveying instruments (an RM4 earth resistance meter and an FM18 fluxgate gradiometer) onto an IBM compatible laptop and processed using GeoPlot version 2.02. The processed data were transferred to Surfer version 6 and prepared for presentation.

The digital archive created by the Cottam project is a research level archive and has been deposited with the ADS. The archive consists of:

- 'Level III' reports covering the stratigraphic sequence
- Fieldwalking, metal detector, geophysical survey reports
- Specialist reports: animal bone, flint, pottery, plant macrofossils
- Geophysics data
- Finds database
- Context database
- CAD files, including a rectified aerial photographic plot
- Colour images of many of the finds

Metadata records were created for the Cottam project as a whole and for individual survey types. Table 3 shows the earth resistance survey documentation for Area 1. The ADS core metadata and the data required for the English Heritage Geophysical Survey database from this survey are listed in Section 5.2.

Acknowledgements
The fieldwork at Cottam was conducted under the auspices of the Department of Archaeology, University of York, and principally funded by the British Academy and the Earthwatch Foundation

Information Type	Description
Survey name	Burrow House Farm, Cottam
Survey index	Area 1 — COT93 — Earth Resistance — CTR1K
Survey purpose	The aim of the survey was to produce a detailed map of sub-surface geophysical anomalies within two sites defined by concentrations of metal finds. One concentration also coincided with a cropmark enclosure. The survey was also to act as a pilot study to assess the relative effectiveness of magnetic and earth resistance techniques in mapping anomalies in this area.

Table 3: Cottam Area 1 Earth Resistance Survey Documentation (continued over the next 3 pages)

Bibliographic references	Richards, J.D. 1999 'Cottam: An Anglian and Anglo-Scandinavian settlement on the Yorkshire Wolds' *Arch J* 156, 1-110 Richards, J.D. 2001 'Anglian and Anglo-Scandinavian Cottam: linking digital publication and archive', *Internet Archaeology*, online: http://intarch.ac.uk/journal/issue10/richards_index.html
Survey keywords	Earth Resistance, Settlement.
Spatial coverage	Area 1: 497565,466700 to 497644,466779
Administrative area	Cottam, East Riding of Yorkshire
Country	England
Solid geology	Chalk
Drift geology	Not reported
Duration	October-December 1994
Weather	Not reported
Soil condition	Not reported
Land-use	Arable
Monument type	Settlement
Monument period	Early medieval
Scheduled Ancient Monument (SAM) number	Not scheduled
Surveyor	Field Archaeology Specialists, Department of Archaeology, King's Manor, York, YO1 7EP
Client	Julian Richards, Department of Archaeology, University of York, King's Manor, York, YO1 7EP
Depositor	Julian Richards, Department of Archaeology, University of York, King's Manor, York, YO1 7EP
Primary archive	Archaeology Data Service Online: http://ads.ahds.ac.uk/catalogue/exc_arch/cottam_ba

Related archives	Digital archive Online: http://ads.ahds.ac.uk/catalogue/exc_arch/cottam_ba/ Physical archive: Hull Museum
Copyright	Julian Richards
Geophysics coordinate system	20m x 20m survey grid laid out with reference to the field boundary to the east.
Georeferencing	The survey area was located in the northern part of the large field to the west of Burrow House Farm.
Coregistration with site grid	
Survey type	Earth resistance
Instrumentation	RM4 Earth Resistance Meter
Probe configuration	PA1 twin-electrode probe array
Probe spacing	0.5m
Area surveyed	0.64 ha
Method of coverage	Regular grid, Zigzag
Traverse separation	1m
Reading interval	1m
Grid size	20m x 20m
Documenting data treatment	The raw data were processed using Geoplot version 2.02. This involved the adjustment of any differences in the average background reading between individual survey grids as well as inconsistencies caused by instrument drift or changing climatic conditions. The data were interpolated to provide a smoother image of the data. The processed data were transferred to Surfer version 6 in which it was prepared for presentation and the resulting grey-scale images were output to a high-definition laser printer.
Report title	Cottam B Geophysical Survey
Report reference number	COT01

Report author	Justin Garner-Lahire
Report holder	Field Archaeology Specialists
Report summary	The survey provided detailed maps of two sites coarsely defined through aerial photography. The results also indicate basic zonation within these sites based on feature density and variations in soil compaction.
List of all filenames	ctr1k.dat resist1.tif resist1.tifw
Explanation of codes used in filenames	ct = Cottam r = Earth resistance 1 = Area 1
Description of file formats	.dat files are Geoplot version 2.02
List of codes used in files	Not applicable
Hardware, software and operating system	IBM compatible PC, Geoplot version 2.02, Surfer version 6
Date of last modification	April 1995
Description of known errors in data	None reported
Indications of known areas of weakness in data	None reported

Table 3: Cottam Area 1 Earth Resistance Survey Documentation

3.12 CASE STUDY: THE LEPTIMINUS GEOPHYSICAL SURVEY

By Damian Robinson and Simon Clarke

Leptiminus was a major port on the eastern seaboard of Tunisia, whose archaeology predominantly dates from the Punic to Byzantine periods. The city was at its apogee in the Roman period, when it was involved in the industrial production of ceramics and in shipment of agricultural produce to the rest of the Roman Empire.

The geophysical survey was a component of a larger research project that also incorporated field survey and selective excavation. The first season of geophysical surveys was undertaken at Leptiminus in the spring of 1995. Additional surveys were carried out in 1996, but are not included in the current archive. The aims of the survey were:

- Surface collection had indicated that Leptiminus was involved in the industrial production of African Red Slip fine ware pottery and amphorae. The primary aim of the geophysical survey was to examine the main areas of kiln debris and ceramic wasters and to investigate the scale of production at Leptiminus. It was hoped that the magnetometer survey could locate potential kiln sites for excavation.

- Early investigations of the city had suggested the existence of a forum and theatre at Leptiminus despite limited archaeological evidence. Hence, the second major aim of the geophysical survey was to investigate the potential monumental core of the city and its internal organisation.

Leptiminus is almost an ideal site for large-scale intra-site geophysical prospection. Today the site is almost entirely open agricultural land, being covered mainly by olive groves. Over fifteen per cent of the city was examined during the two seasons of work, which sampled a wide range of city environments: coastal and inland; city core and suburbs; industrial, public and residential areas.

In the field the geophysical data were downloaded from the surveying instrument (a Geoscan FM36) onto an IBM compatible laptop computer using Geoplot 1.4. The raw data files from Geoplot (.dat) were then renamed as .gpt files, using a standard file-naming convention and imported into Contors (Contors files being named .dat again) for balancing and initial data processing. The data were then viewed using spike removal and bicubic interpolation. The images were screen captured and pasted into PhotoShop and then saved as Uncompressed Tiff files using a file-naming convention (e.g. AM_-5-8c.tif = Area A, magnetometer, -5 to 8 nT range [as used in the Contors display] and 'c' for 'captured'). The screen images were then cropped to display only the area of the survey and saved with a filename omitting the ending 'c': AM_-5-8.tif. These survey images were imported as raster backdrops into AutoCAD (R14) for georegistration and the generation of vectorised overlay interpretations of the geophysical anomalies. The geo-information was transcribed from detailed field notes. These CAD files were then exported as .dxf and imported into the field survey GIS for further data analysis.

The digital archive created by the Leptiminus geophysical survey project is a research level archive and has been deposited with the ADS. It will be released to coincide with, and support, the final publication of the survey (Clarke and Robinson *forthcoming*). The archive consists of:

- geophysical survey metadata
- raw Geoplot files
- semi-processed Contors files
- archival (uncompressed .tiff) raster images of each geophysical survey area
- dissemination (.jpeg) raster images of each geophysical survey area
- vector interpretations of the geophysical anomalies
- archive text reports and supporting documentation
- images of Leptiminus and the geophysical survey

The time lag between the completion of the geophysical survey and the publication of the larger Leptiminus project has altered the archiving strategy. The production of the digital archive was never originally envisaged and it is fortuitous that the raw Geoplot data could be salvaged after the destruction of the original survey laptop and the corruption of a set of back-up disks. All of the images were re-created in archival preservation file formats. The survey metadata had to be retrospectively created but the majority of the documentation was retrieved from the two end-of-season reports and earlier versions of the final project report. The archiving process involved both the limited creation of new digital data and gathering together old data.

ACKNOWLEDGEMENTS

The geophysical survey at Leptiminus was funded by grants from the British Academy and the University of Michigan. The Department of Archaeological Sciences at the University of Bradford provided equipment and technical advice.

Project Documentation	
Survey name	Leptiminus Geophysical Survey Project
Survey index	LAm — Area A Magnetometer Survey
Survey purpose	To examine an area with a high concentration of kiln debris and ceramic wasters
Survey keywords	Leptiminus, Roman, city, Geophysical survey, kiln, African red slip, amphorae, ceramic wasters
Spatial coverage	Withheld
Country	Tunisia
Duration	29th April to 1st May 1995
Weather	Hot and sunny
Soil condition	Dry
Land-use	Small fields of olive trees
Monument type	Ancient city
Monument period	Punic, Roman, Byzantine
Geophysical survey directors	Damian Robinson, Simon Clarke
Geophysical surveyors	Robert McNaught, Mark Williams, Matthew Braithwaite

Table 4: Leptiminus Area A Magnetometer Survey Documentation (continued over the next 4 pages)

Client	Leptiminus Archaeological Project
Depositor	Dr Damian Robinson Department of Archaeology University of York
Primary archive	Archaeology Data Service online: http://ads.ahds.ac.uk/catalogue/
Copyright	Damian Robinson and Simon Clarke
Geophysical Survey	
Survey type	Magnetometer
Instrumentation	Geoscan FM36 Fluxgate Gradiometer
Area surveyed	35 grids (20m x 20m) – approximately 1.4 ha
Method of coverage	Regular grid
Traverse separation	1m
Reading interval	1m
Sampling position	0.5m in both directions from the south-west grid cell
Grid size	20m x 20m
Accuracy: spatial	Some variation of grid layout occurred across the survey area: grids further from the baseline are up to 1 metre out due to the uneven nature of the terrain and the difficulties in setting out grids in olive groves. The estimated positional accuracy within the grids is 0.1m
Accuracy: readings	Automatic trigger while walking, 0.1 nano tesla sensitivity
Data Recording	
Grid layout and list of grid names	The grid layout is documented in the Contors report file LAm.rep and individual data grid files are named according to the acquisition sequence, example: 'AM2.dat'
Grid size	20m x 20m
Resolution	1m x 1m

Survey direction	Parallel lines, walked from West to East, starting from the north-west corner of each grid. Consecutive lines were recorded further South
Line sequence	All lines were surveyed in the same direction ('parallel')
Drift value	Recorded as the 401st value in each data file
Dummy value	-900
Documenting Data Treatment	
Processing steps	1. Data downloaded from machine to field computer using Geoplot version 1.4 2. Geoplot .dat files renamed as .gpt files 3. .gpt files imported into Contors to produce Contors .dat files 4. Data viewed in Contors using spike removal and bicubic interpolation 5. Images screen-captured and saved as Uncompressed Tiff for preservation 6. Images processed using PhotoShop 7. Images imported as raster backdrops into AutoCAD for geo-registration and the generation of vectorised interpretations of the geophysical anomalies
Report Documentation	
Report title	Leptiminus Area A: a brief report
Report number	LeptA-01
Report author	Simon Clarke and Damian Robinson
Report holder	Damian Robinson
Report summary	Geophysical surveys in Area A indicated that the banks of the Oued es Souk were lined with buildings, which are most likely dwellings with associated cisterns. Magnetometer surveys revealed a line of possible kilns running SW to NE across the line of the survey and at an angle to the line of the probable dwellings.

Digital Data Documentation	
List of all file names	Contors data files – AM1.dat to AM35.dat Contors report - LAm.rep Image files – AM_–5-8.tif CAD file – Area_A_Features.dxf Text files – Area_A_Metadata.doc, Area_A_a_brief_report.doc
Explanation of codes used in filenames	Contors files AM1 = Area A, magnetometer, grid1 Image files AM_–5-8 = Area A, magnetometer, -5 to 8 nT range used in the Contors display
Description of file formats	Contors .dat files for data Contors .rep for grid location information
Hardware, software and operating system used	1. Data downloaded directly from instruments into an IBM compatible laptop (Windows 3.1) using Geoplot V1.4 2. Contors for DOS used for geophysical processing 3. PhotoShop used for image processing 4. AutoCAD (R14) used for vectorised interpretations of the geophysical anomalies
Date of last modification	Initial survey and write-up in 1995. Data were re-examined in March 2001.

Table 4: Leptiminus Area A Magnetometer Survey Documentation

Section 4: Digital Archiving of Archaeological Geophysical Data

Previous sections explained that the archive of an archaeological geophysical project consists not only of the measured data, interpretations, images and reports but also of the project documentation to describe data and work. This section will discuss issues related to the archiving of such resources.

4.1 INTRODUCTION

Archaeological geophysics is in a special position with respect to archiving because its data are collected, manipulated, and analysed in a digital environment. Indeed the digital record is the only source of precious research materials. With the ever-increasing pace of change in computer hardware and software, however, in a few years' time these data may be lost forever. The best strategy for long-term preservation of archaeological data in digital formats is for them to be systematically collected, maintained and made accessible to users operating in very different computing environments.

Digital archiving is different from traditional archiving. Traditional archiving practice seeks to preserve physical objects (e.g. artefacts, samples, paper, photographs, microfilm) that carry information. Digital archiving is about preserving *information* regardless of the media on which that information is stored. This is because diskettes and other magnetic and optical media degrade, and software and hardware change rapidly: the physical media on which digital data are stored are impermanent.

This problem has been effectively demonstrated through work carried out to rescue the contents of the Newham Museum Archaeological Service digital archive (Austin *et al.* 2001). The Archaeological Service was closed in 1998 and although the physical remains are still curated by the London boroughs of Newham, Redbridge and Waltham Forest, the digital archive was passed to the ADS. The digital archive represented all the work that was digitised during Archaeological Service fieldwork, and post-excavation analysis, along with project designs over a period of about ten years. This archive was delivered to the ADS on 230 floppy disks containing over 6000 files and totalling over 130 Mb of data. The data were, for the most part, in archaic formats and used proprietary software, and significant time and effort were required to rescue the majority of these files. Unfortunately around 10–15% of the files are still inaccessible and the data that they contain are effectively lost. Another problem was that the archive was inadequately documented and it was often difficult to reconstruct which files went with which project. As a result there are a number of 'orphaned' data sets, including several geophysical survey projects, which have been rescued but have little re-use potential.

The Newham Museum Archaeological Service digital archive had two main problems:

1   data held in non-preservation file formats, i.e. proprietary file formats that have gone out of use

2   documentation was missing for both data and projects

The Newham digital archive is probably a typical example of the digital information resources of archaeological units. There are many archaeology units with archives of files in redundant formats, which contain unexplained coding and are in unknown states of completion, without explicit information relating them to sites(*cf.* Condron *et al.* 1999). The files may also be kept on unsuitable media under poor conditions of storage. In short, there may be large amounts of 'archived' archaeological information which can never be accessed again.

The Newham Museum Service digital archive is a depressing and salutary tale. It was developed as a working tool to help the Service undertake, write up and manage its archaeological projects. In this respect the archive was fit for the purpose for which it was developed. The concept of digital project archiving was still in its infancy when the Newham archive was developed. As there were no published strategies or methodologies in place to ensure the effective preservation of the data, the poor condition of the Newham archive is understandable.

This *Guide* has been developed to offer preservation strategies for archaeological geophysics data, as it is clear that the road to long-term preservation begins not at the end of a project but at its beginning.

4.2 PLANNING FOR THE CREATION OF DIGITAL DATA

From the moment a project begins, careful thought must go into the digital archive that will be produced. Planning should include:

- **Preparing a project design** that documents the tasks necessary for the successful completion of the project at its outset and includes a summary of the types of digital data that will be created. It is important to update this documentation throughout the life of the project.

- **Defining and documenting areas of responsibility** for creating and managing digital files at all stages of their life.

- **Planning the file formats that will be used** for both the secure archiving and the dissemination of data. The formats used for these two activities may be different.

- **Checking any guidelines or standards** recommended by the digital archive facility destined to receive the files and ensuring these are followed. If local guidelines do not exist, it is recommended that the guidelines in this document are followed and that the ADS is consulted for up-to-date information.

4.2.1 File-naming conventions

Digital files should be given meaningful titles that reflect their content. It is recommended that standard file-naming conventions and directory structures should be used from the beginning of a project. If possible, consistent conventions should be used for all projects, for example:

- Reserve the 3-letter file extension for application-specific codes, e.g. PDF, DOC, TIF.
- Identify the activity or project in the file name, e.g. use a unique reference number, project number or project name.
- Include the version number in the file name where necessary.
- Files generated under DOS must use standard 8-character file names with 3-character file extensions. Longer and more meaningful file names may be used under Windows, Apple and Unix environments.

4.2.2 Version control

It is extremely important to maintain strict version control when working with files, especially with geophysical data which may be saved in composite or other formats and processed using a series of different treatments.

There are three common strategies for providing version control: file-naming conventions, standard headers listing creation dates and version numbers, or file logs. It is important to record, where practical, every change to a file no matter how small the change. Versions that are no longer needed should be weeded out, after making sure that adequate back-up files have been created.

4.2.3 Images

Original images, plans or other graphical materials should be digitised or scanned using the highest quality data capture to create archival quality data files. These files may be compressed for dissemination purposes, by techniques that often depend on degrading data quality. It may be advisable to create and store multiple versions of each file for different purposes (see Table 8 Section 6.2). The originals from which the digital data sets were created may still be useful and a documentary archive should be consulted to establish whether this information should be preserved in paper format.

4.3 STORING DIGITAL DATA SETS

During the working life of a project, digital data may be created on the hard disks of stand alone PCs, on laptop computers or on network drives, and data may be acquired on floppy disks, backup-tapes, CD-ROMS or other electronic media. While work is in progress digital files should be transferred to locations where they will be routinely backed up, e.g. files should be copied from floppy disks onto a network drive.

Fireproof and anti-magnetic facilities are extremely important for the safe storage of digital media, and back-up versions should be stored separated from original media. It is recommended that data documentation should be included with the storage media. It is also important to create a separate record of the locations where files are stored and how they are labelled.

4.3.1 Secure backing-up

Back-up is the familiar task of ensuring that there is an emergency copy (or a snap shot) of all data held separately in case of damage to the original data (by accident or through a disaster). For a small project this may mean a single file held on a floppy disk or on a network; for a larger project or data set it may involve complex procedures involving disaster planning, with fireproof cupboards, off-site copies and daily, weekly and monthly refreshing. Such back-up strategies are important in the lifespan of the project but are not the same as long-term archiving of the data (see Section 4.4).

The *'Grandparent-Parent-Child' strategy* is the most widely used back-up procedure. The system works by rotating full and partial back-ups on each day of the week or month:

- The *'Parent'* is the most recent full back-up and contains a snap-shot of the system at the start of a week.

- *'Children'* are normally daily back-ups containing only the changes to the system made on that day. These are generally recycled every time a new Parent is created.

- The *'Grandparent'* is a complete snap-shot of the system that is taken every month. This should be stored in perpetuity and would not normally be recycled. This back-up can be brought out in moments of real crisis.

The system can be tailored to individual requirements. For a small data set, or one that changes infrequently, such regular copying may be excessive and the time periods may be expanded or contracted as necessary. It is best practice that the weekly and monthly back-ups are stored away from the office, preferably in a secure, fireproof, anti-magnetic environment.

It is important to *validate* the back-up copies to ensure that all formatting and important data have been accurately preserved. Creating back-ups is advisable when a project is complete or dormant, prior to any major changes, or if files are large enough to cause handling difficulties on the network. Each back-up should be clearly labelled, and its location should be logged.

4.3.2 Virus checking and other issues

Viruses are self-executing programs that enter a computing system hidden inside harmless programs or files disguised to encourage unsuspecting users to install them. Once in a system, they replicate themselves and carry out operations which range from the invisible to the vaguely irritating to the absolutely devastating. Trojans are programs that appear to have useful or desirable features that entice people to install or download them but they actually exist to do damage. Trojans do not replicate themselves and once the damage has been repaired they do not return. Worms are similar to viruses in that they replicate themselves and often interfere with the normal use of a computer or a program. Worms differ in that they exist as separate entities; they do not attach themselves to other files or programs.

While the damage caused by viruses, trojans and worms can be great, the actual risk is less than some would believe. Experience suggests that much of the damage blamed on viruses and trojans is actually the result of poor management. There is, however, a constant and real, if minor, risk from genuine, malicious programs, which because the programs are invisible, may be transmitted unawares by the most innocent of sources.

There are some basic steps which can be taken to avoid viruses, trojans and worms:

- Install anti-virus software on the computer, and make sure that it is routinely upgraded (every month) because new viruses and trojans are constantly being designed and older software might not identify these.
- Be suspicious of any unsolicited programs or files, particularly from unwanted email.
- Do not download any more software from the Internet than is strictly necessary.
- Scan all files received with the appropriate software, even those from close colleagues or friends.
- Refrain from forwarding emails labelled 'Virus Warning' or similar. Most of these are hoaxes and some are viruses. Consult the lists maintained by anti-virus software houses before forwarding these messages.
- When buying software look for an anti-virus guarantee.
- Have a back-up strategy in place should the worst happen.

4.4 DIGITAL ARCHIVING STRATEGIES

Digital archiving strategies do not, and should not, rely on the preservation of a single disk, tape, or CD-ROM. The essence of digital archiving lies in one of three strategies (Beagrie and Greenstein 1998):

- **Migration** of information from older hardware and software systems to newer systems. This is the strategy recommended for most archaeological applications.

- **Emulation** of older hardware/software systems in newer systems. This is technically challenging, extremely expensive and becomes increasingly difficult as current technology becomes ever more remote from the original systems employed. Emulation is consequently not recommended for archaeological archives.

- **Complete preservation of old hardware and software systems**. This costly high-risk strategy is not justifiable unless data cannot be migrated and are of substantial importance.

Digital archiving in archaeology should revolve around a policy of controlled data migration. There are four main activities required for successful digital archiving with this strategy:

1   data refreshment
2   data migration
3   documentation
4   data management tools.

4.4.1 Data refreshment

Data refreshment is the act of copying information from one medium to the next as the original medium nears the end of its reliable lifespan. Research into the lifespan of both magnetic and optical media has shown that the former can be safe for 5–10 years and the latter may survive more than 30. However, technology changes much more quickly and digital media are far more likely to become unreadable as a result of changing technology than through media degradation.

For example, ten years ago many archaeologists collected information on 3-inch Amstrad diskettes. These diskettes are completely unreadable by PC machines. The data cannot be accessed on a PC except by connecting a surviving Amstrad to a network or by connecting a 3.5-inch disk drive to its serial port. Even then, the data need to be exported into a standard format such as ASCII, as Amstrads use a different operating system to PCs. If archaeologists had refreshed their data from 3-inch Amstrad diskettes to 5.25-inch disks and then to 3.5-inch disks, these digital data would still be accessible and safe.

Computer software changes even more rapidly than computer hardware. Data files that have been created in the proprietary format of a particular software package may not be retrievable in future. The software company may change the formats used in subsequent versions of the package, or may cease trading and the datafile may not be accessible by software produced by other companies. However, there are file formats that have been earmarked as industry standards or open formats that, while losing some of the original versatility, may nonetheless allow files to be imported into other software.

4.4.2 Data migration

Data migration is even more important than data refreshment. Migration is the act of copying digital information from one format or structure into another. One example is copying old flat-field database files into a newer relational database. The functionality of a flat-field database can be maintained in a relational database structure. In this case, migration also enables improvements in functionality as the data handling and retrieval capabilities of relational databases can be drawn upon.

The definitions of some file formats allow a large number of options that may be interpreted differently by the various software manufacturers. This can result in incompatibilities between different packages when data are migrated, even when a 'standard' format has been used. Examples of such formats are DXF for Computer-Aided Design (CAD) files and TIFF for images. In these cases the most basic export options should be used and archival guidelines respected. For example, the ADS recommends only uncompressed TIFF files (see Section 6.2, table 8).

In order for a digital archivist to migrate digital information successfully, it is necessary to understand fully the structure of the data and how different parts relate to one another. It is important to retain the original media until the migrated data has been validated.

4.4.3 Documentation

Data migration thus relies on the third activity: *documentation*. No digital archivist can successfully preserve data that are not fully documented, because at every step of data migration information can be lost. This leaves archivists with two options: migrating data from one format and then double-checking each entry manually, or requiring thorough documentation of the data at the time of archiving so migration can be carefully planned and tested in advance.

4.4.4 Data management tools

As already noted, digital data need to be regularly refreshed and migrated. Files that have been altered should move naturally into a localised back-up strategy but where a deep storage facility is also employed (a preferred archival strategy where files are additionally stored in a remote and specialised repository), active intervention may be required for updating and version control. Thus digital archives need to be actively managed and data management tools such as Electronic Document Management systems may be used. These are usually databases that, ideally, will flag dates and automatically inform the system manager when files need attention.

Section 5: Resource Discovery

5.1 ACCESS AND RE-USE

The potential audience for archaeological geophysical survey data is diverse. Professional geophysicists or researchers may, for example, want to find information about the results from surveys that used particular equipment on a specific geology, so that they can test new data processing and interpretation tools. Archaeologists may want to know about surveys undertaken on a particular type of archaeological site or in a certain area. There are also uses for geophysical data to support courses in university departments and schools, by students and also by interested members of the public. However, the *Survey of Archaeological Archives* (Swain 1998, 43–5) concluded that archives containing archaeological data were grossly under-utilised.

One of the reasons given by the Swain report for this limited use of archives was the difficulty in finding information about the location of archives and particularly about their contents. In the case of geophysical survey data, the results from *Strategies for Digital Data* (Condron *et al.* 1999, 29–32) show that this material is often retained by its creators or deposited with national agencies or local authorities. The task is therefore to make information available that helps to discover these resources through the increasing number of Internet gateways and search engines. The Internet is an important means of finding resources and may also be used to retrieve geophysical data archives wherever they are held.

Access to archaeological geophysical archives is important because:

- It facilitates communication within archaeology about work that has been undertaken thus:
  - helping to avoid duplication of effort,
  - providing resources to test and develop new techniques for data treatment and analysis,
  - enabling new research with already existing data sources
- Sharing data also helps in their preservation – the more formats a data set is copied into, the greater the chance of its surviving.

5.2 METADATA AS AN AID TO RESOURCE DISCOVERY

In order to find relevant data in an archive it needs to be indexed in a suitable way. A library catalogue, for example, uses the names of authors, book titles and keywords to find the corresponding works in the shelves. This index-information is often referred to as 'metadata', which means 'data describing the original information'. In Section 3, a large number of items were listed, which together describe an individual geophysical survey. To find the survey (and its associated measurements) in an archive or database some of these descriptors will be used as metadata to search for the original resource (e.g. 'Survey name', 'Survey type').

The specific selection of descriptors that are used as metadata will depend on the level of detail with which an archive is to be searched. This can be illustrated with three examples as, at present, different levels of metadata about archaeological geophysical surveys are being made available through the English Heritage Geophysical Survey Database, ArcHSearch (the ADS online catalogue) and through the Arts and Humanities Data Service Gateway:

1   The metadata that are recorded in the English Heritage Geophysical Survey Database (EH GSdb) enable detailed resource discovery of geophysical surveys. This allows very specific queries to locate a resource, for example searches for 'all magnetometer surveys over limestone' or 'all earth resistance surveys of Roman villas'. To achieve this a fair number of descriptors from Section 3 are used as metadata to index the archive.

2   ArcHSearch describes archaeological resources at a more general level to accommodate a wide range of different types of archaeological data, for example CAD files, SMR data, CBA Research Reports and so on. Therefore, fewer of the geophysical survey descriptors are registered as metadata. Thus searches in ArcHSearch are at a more general level, for example 'all geophysical surveys in Cheshire' or 'all information relating to Fishbourne Palace'.

3   The Arts and Humanities Data Service Gateway describes resources from across the arts and humanities using generic metadata. This allows searches across collections held on different websites by different data services. Thus searches in the AHDS gateway are more general again, for example 'all resources relating to Chester' or 'all resources relating to Shakespeare'.

Thus different levels of metadata may be made available through various resource discovery tools. The remaining descriptors from Section 3 are then regarded as 'documentation' forming part of the archived resource. Project managers are advised to create metadata about each geophysical survey and its digital archive, and make them available on a collection level as soon as possible following the completion of a project.

Data exchange agreements are in place between the ADS and English Heritage's GSdb. This means that, if organisations provide the ADS with metadata (including the additional metadata required for EH GSdb), the ADS will forward these to English Heritage. Similarly, all entries and additions to the EH GSdb will be available as metadata through the ADS and, where possible, links will be made to the survey information held by English Heritage. Such data exchange ensures that a comprehensive view of existing archaeological geophysical data is available for the whole community.

5.2.1 ArcHSearch: data in the ADS collections

ArcHSearch, the ADS online catalogue contains over 350,000 metadata records relating to sites, monuments, surveys and other archaeological interventions in the British Isles and internationally. These index records have been supplied to the ADS both by the curators of excavation and fieldwork archives (the NMRs, SMRs and museums) and by the creators of digital archives (including contracting and consultancy units, research projects and others). On completion of fieldwork, responsible organisations are encouraged to deposit metadata with the ADS describing the work that has taken place. Table 5 shows an example of an ADS metadata record for a geophysical survey; a description of each metadata element can be found in Table 9, Appendix 2 and also on the ADS web-site (Online: http://ads.ahds.ac.uk/project/metadata.html).

In some cases, organisations also deposit geophysical (and other archaeological) data sets. Each of these data sets is related to a metadata record that was provided as part of the project documentation. This allows users to identify archived resources before down-loading relevant data. In other cases, the metadata record in ArcHSearch provides a link to data that are held on a web-site maintained by another organisation, for example the RCAHMS.

The metadata included in ArcHSearch are listed below. Names in brackets indicate the metadata labels which are used by ArcHSearch.

* Survey name (Name of Resource)
* Survey index (Resource Identifiers)
* Survey purpose (Description)
* Survey keywords (Intervention Type/Subject)
* Spatial coverage (Map Reference)
* Administrative area (Place/Parish/District or Unitary Authority/County)
* Country (Country)
* Duration (Project Dates)
* Monument period (Period)
* Depositor (Responsible for work)
* Related archives (Paper/microfilm archive: Location/Contents)
* Copyright (Copyright)

Information type	Scope note
Survey name	Burrow House Farm, Cottam
Survey index	Area 1 - COT93 - Earth Resistance - CTR1K
Survey purpose	The aim of the survey was to produce a detailed map of sub-surface geophysical anomalies within two sites defined by concentrations of metal finds. One concentration also coincided with a cropmark enclosure. The survey was also to act as a pilot study to assess the relative effectiveness of magnetic and earth resistance techniques in mapping anomalies in this area.

Table 5: An example of a metadata record for a geophysical survey
from ArcHSearch (continued over the page)

Survey keywords	Earth Resistance, Settlement.
Spatial coverage	Area 1: 497565,466700 to 497644,466779
Administrative area	Cottam, East Riding of Yorkshire
Country	England
Duration	October-December 1994
Monument period	Early medieval
Depositor	Julian Richards, Department of Archaeology, University of York, King's Manor, York, YO1 7EP
Related archives	Digital archive online: http://ads.ahds.ac.uk/catalogue/exc_arch/cottam _ba/ Physical archive: Hull Museum
Copyright	Julian Richards

Table 5: An example of a metadata record for a geophysical survey from ArcHSearch (continued)

Access to the ADS catalogue and archive is regulated by strict copyright statements and access agreements (see the ADS Copyright and Liability Statement (Online: http://ads.ahds.ac.uk/ copy.html) and the AHDS Common Access Agreement (Online: http://ads.ahds.ac.uk/cap.html)). In cases where the survey or associated details are sensitive, more limited metadata may be deposited. For example, where there are concerns in relation to site security locational information may be made available at low precision (see *Spatial Coverage*, Section 3.2). More detailed information may then be released to authorised enquirers only.

5.2.2 The English Heritage Geophysical Survey Database

The English Heritage Geophysical Survey Database (EH GSdb) (Online: http://www.eng-h.gov.uk/SDB/) was specifically designed to hold information on archaeological geophysical surveys. The database includes similar metadata to ArcHSearch and Table 6 shows an example of an English Heritage metadata record for a geophysical survey. A description of each metadata element can be found in Tables 9 and 10, Appendix 2 and is also documented on the English Heritage website (Online: http://www.eng-h.gov.uk).

The EH GSdb metadata are listed below with EH metadata labels in brackets:

- Survey name (Project Title)
- Survey index
- Survey purpose (Purpose of Survey)
- Bibliographic references (Bibliographic References)
- Spatial coverage (Grid Reference)
- Administrative area (County/Unitary Authority)
- Country
- Solid geology (Solid Geology)
- Drift geology (Drift Geology)
- Duration (Occurred between)
- Weather
- Land-use (Land use)
- Monument type (Monuments covered)
- Monument period
- Scheduled Ancient Monument (SAM) number
- Surveyor (Surveyor/Personnel)
- Client (Client)
- Depositor
- Primary archive
- Related archives
- Copyright
- Survey keywords (Archaeological Feature Classifications)
- Survey type (Geophysical Techniques Used)
- Instrumentation (Instrument Type/Instrument make)
- Probe configuration (Electrode configuration)
- Probe spacing (Electrode separation)
- Area surveyed (Area Surveyed)
- Method of coverage
- Traverse separation (Traverse Separation)
- Reading interval (Reading Interval)
- Additional remarks (for data collection) (Comments on Survey)
- Report title (Report Title)
- Report reference number (Report Number)
- Report author (Author/Report Date)
- Report holder (Report held by)
- Report summary (Synopsis of report content)

5.2.3 The AHDS Gateway: data in the ADS collections

Through its service providers, the AHDS manages high-quality data resources including the Archaeology Data Service, the History Data Service, the Oxford Text Archive and the Performing Arts Data Service. The AHDS Gateway acts as a 'union catalogue' through which

Information type	Scope note
Survey name	Burrow House Farm, Cottam
Survey index	Area 1 — COT93 — Earth Resistance — CTR1K
Survey purpose	The aim of the survey was to produce a detailed map of sub-surface geophysical anomalies within two sites defined by concentrations of metal finds. One concentration also coincided with a cropmark enclosure. The survey was also to act as a pilot study to assess the relative effectiveness of magnetic and earth resistance techniques in mapping anomalies in this area.
Bibliographic references	Richards, J.D. 1999 'Cottam: An Anglian and Anglo-Scandinavian settlement on the Yorkshire Wolds' *Arch J* 156, 1-110 Richards, J.D. 2001 'Anglian and Anglo-Scandinavian Cottam: linking digital publication and archive', *Internet Archaeology*, Online: http://intarch.ac.uk/journal/issue10/richards_index.html
Survey keywords	Earth Resistance, Settlement.
Spatial coverage	Area 1: 497565,466700 to 497644,466779
Administrative area	Cottam, East Riding of Yorkshire
Country	England
Solid geology	Chalk
Drift geology	Not reported
Duration	October-December 1994
Weather	Not reported

Table 6: An example of a metadata record from the English Heritage Geophysical Survey Database (continued over the next 2 pages)

Land-use	Arable
Monument type	Settlement
Monument period	Early medieval
Scheduled Ancient Monument (SAM) number	Not scheduled
Surveyor	Field Archaeology Specialists, Department of Archaeology, King's Manor, York, YO1 7EP
Client	Julian Richards, Department of Archaeology, University of York, King's Manor, York, YO1 7EP
Depositor	Julian Richards, Department of Archaeology, University of York, King's Manor, York, YO1 7EP
Primary archive	Archaeology Data Service, Online: http://ads.ahds.ac.uk/catalogue/exc_arch/cottam_ba/
Related Archives	Digital archive: Online: http://ads.ahds.ac.uk/catalogue/exc_arch/cottam_ba/ Physical archive: Hull Museum
Copyright	Julian Richards
Survey type	Earth Resistance
Instrumentation	RM4 Earth Resistance Meter
Probe configuration	PA1 twin-electrode probe array
Probe spacing	0.5m
Area surveyed	0.64 ha
Method of coverage	Regular grid, Zigzag
Traverse separation	1m
Reading Interval	1m
Additional remarks	None

Report title	Cottam B Geophysical Survey
Report reference number	COT01
Report author	Justin Garner-Lahire
Report holder	Field Archaeology Specialists
Report summary	The survey provided detailed maps of two sites coarsely defined through aerial photography. The results also indicate basic zonation within these sites based on feature density and variations in soil compaction.

Table 6: An example of a metadata record from the English Heritage Geophysical Survey Database

Information type	Scope note
Service provider	Archaeology Data Service
Survey name	Burrow House Farm, Cottam
Duration	1993-1995
Depositor	J.D. Richards (University of York)
Copyright	J.D. Richards
Survey index	1
Survey keywords	Geophysical Survey, Settlement, Cottam, Wolds
Format	text/html, DAT, TIF

Table 7: An example of a metadata record from the AHDS catalogue

users can search collections held by all of the service providers. The AHDS Gateway serves to point users towards the specialist collections held by its service providers.

A description of the AHDS Gateway and each metadata element can be found on the AHDS website (Online: http://ahds.ac.uk).

The AHDS metadata are given below with the AHDS metadata labels in brackets:

- Service provider (e.g. ADS)
- Survey name (Title)

- Duration (Date)
- Depositor (Creator)
- Copyright (Copyright)
- Survey index (i.e. the depositor's identifier)
- Survey keywords (Subject)
- Format (i.e. the format in which the data are held)

Section 6: Depositing Archaeological Geophysical Data in a Digital Archive

6.1 GUIDELINES FOR DEPOSITING DIGITAL ARCHIVES

Some guidelines about digital archiving are already mandatory for certain sectors within the discipline of archaeology. For example, museum curators working in UK museums that are accredited by the Museums and Galleries Commission should adhere to the MGC (1992) and SMA (1993; 1995) guidelines for archive access, deposition, recording, and storage. Archaeologists funded by Historic Scotland must adhere to *Publication and Archiving of Archaeological Projects* (Historic Scotland 1996a see also 1996b) and the *Guidelines for Archiving of Archaeological Projects* (RCAHMS 1996). Projects funded by English Heritage must conform to the Guidelines known as MAP2 (EH 1991). Projects in Wales should be aware of the developing strategy for archaeology in Wales (Cadw and RCAHMW 1998). Archaeologists creating digital data with funds received from the Arts and Humanities Research Board, British Academy, Council for British Archaeology, Leverhulme Trust, Natural Environment Research Council, Society of Antiquaries of London, or the Wellcome Trust should deposit digital archives with the Archaeology Data Service (ADS 1998).

Special archiving requirements are often included in project designs or specifications that vary on a case-by-case basis (e.g. Northamptonshire Heritage 1998). In West Yorkshire, for example, provision for archiving digital fieldwork data is ensured through planning conditions.

Most existing archive repositories are aware of, but have not yet confronted, the challenges of preserving digital data sets. Indeed the recent *Survey of Archaeological Archives in England* (Swain 1998, 47) concluded that 'most museums do not have the correct technology to store, access and curate in the long-term those archives for which computer files play an important part'.

It should be the responsibility of those managing archaeological resources in a region to liase over how best to manage the digital resource for their area (whether locally or through an agency such as the ADS) and then articulate this to contractors. Geophysical surveys generally take place as part of a project involving other archaeological investigative techniques. We recommend that, when considering where to deposit the geophysical data and metadata from such a project, fieldworkers should consult the museum, National Monuments Record, SMR, or other archive repository that will receive the rest of the project archive about their digital archiving policy. This consultation should take place at the start of a project so that the appropriate procedures for depositing archives can be incorporated into the project plan. If in doubt about what to do with digital archives, project workers are advised to contact the ADS for information.

6.2 DEPOSITING GEOPHYSICAL DATA WITH THE ARCHAEOLOGY DATA SERVICE

The ADS archives, disseminates and catalogues high-quality digital resources of long-term interest to archaeologists. Its geographical remit is to provide digital archiving facilities for all areas of the world in which UK archaeologists have research interests. The ADS collections' scope is thus international.

The ADS acknowledges the considerable benefit to both depositors and users of an effective and rigorous process of peer review of materials proposed for accessioning. In order to assist the ADS to evaluate data sets and maintain the rigorous standards necessary for the effective development of a quality resource base, a *Collections Evaluation Working Party* has been set up.

Data resources that are offered for deposit to the ADS will be evaluated to:

- Assess their intellectual content and the level of potential interest in their re-use.
- Evaluate how (even whether) they may viably be managed, preserved, and distributed to potential secondary users.
- Determine the presence or absence of another suitable archival home.

Whereas the first form of evaluation involves assessment of the content of a data resource, the second focuses more on data structure and format, and on the nature and completeness of any documentation supplied. The third evaluation criterion is intended to prevent duplication of digital archiving efforts within the archaeological community, and to preserve the integrity of existing digital archives. Such evaluation is essential to determine how best to manage a digital resource for the purpose of preservation and secondary re-use, and also to determine what costs may be involved in accessioning and migrating the digital resource. For further information please refer to the ADS Collections Policy (Online: http://ads.ahds.ac.uk/project/collpol3.html)

6.2.1 Deposit formats

In the last few years many data formats have appeared that are intended to make data exchange and migration easier. Some of these formats are proprietary (i.e. they are marketed by a single company) but many are open standards that are independent of the software that is used. In general, open data formats are preferred for digital preservation. Unfortunately, software manufacturers use open file formats but occasionally change them slightly so as to be less than 100% compatible with other software manufacturers. It is best to enquire with a digital archiving body in the planning stages of any project to check if there are any concerns with the anticipated file formats.

The format in which data will be deposited depends on the type of information that is contained within. The Archaeology Data Service recommends the file formats outlined in Table 8 for delivery to the ADS, long-term preservation and for Internet dissemination. 'Delivery' formats pertain to the file types that will be accepted by the ADS as a component of a deposit. Where necessary these delivery file formats will be migrated into a 'Preservation' format for long-term storage and may also be converted to a 'Dissemination' format for delivery over the Internet. Dissemination formats may also include widely used proprietary formats such as Microsoft Word and Adobe Acrobat files for texts and jpeg for images, which may have no long-term preservation potential. For raw geophysical data, the ADS is able to accept files in Geoplot, InSite or Contors format. If none of these is available, xyz format

Data Type	Delivery Formats	Preservation Formats	Dissemination Formats
CAD	DXF, DWG plus some native file formats	DXF, DWG	DXF, DWG, DWF
Databases	ASCII delimited text, MS Access (up to Ver. 2000), Paradox (up to Ver. 8), DBF	ASCII delimited text	ASCII delimited text
Geophysics	Geoplot, InSite, Contors, plain text (data + control info), AGF	AGF, plain text (data + control info)	AGF, plain text (data + control info)
GIS	ArcInfo export, ArcInfo ungen, ArcInfo shapefile, DXF + DWG, ArcView (up to Ver. 3), MIF/MID, NTFF, SDTF, MOSS, VDF	ArcInfo, DXF, DWG	ArcInfo, DXF, DWG
Images	Uncompressed TIFF, GeoTIFF, BMP, PNG	Uncompressed TIFF	Uncompressed TIFF, BMP, JPEG
Spreadsheets	ASCII delimited text, Excel (up to V. 2000), Lotus123, Quattro Pro	ASCII delimited text	ASCII delimited text
Texts	ASCII text, RTF, HTML, PDF, Postscript, LaTeX, ODA, SGML, TeX, Word, WordPerfect	ASCII text, HTML	ASCII text, HTML, PDF, Word

Table 8: Delivery, Preservation and Dissemination file formats

ASCII files may be used (see Section 3.5). However, the preferred format is AGF (Schmidt forthcoming) since it is independent of any proprietary software.

6.2.2 Contacting the Archaeology Data Service

Please feel free to contact the ADS directly if you have any questions or concerns.
Archaeology Data Service
University of York
King's Manor
York YO1 7EP
Telephone: +44 (0)1904 433 954
Fax: +44 (0)1904 433 939
Email: info@ads.ahds.ac.uk
http://ads.ahds.ac.uk/

Glossary

Access	A widely-used database package from Microsoft.
ADS	The Archaeology Data Service (Online: http://ads.ahds.ac.uk/).
Adobe Acrobat	Publishing software that allows the production of standardised document files (file extension .pdf)
AGF	Archaeological Grid Format.
AHDS	The Arts and Humanities Data Service (Online: http://ahds.ac.uk/).
AML	Ancient Monuments Laboratory.
ARC/Info	A commercial GIS package from ESRI widely used within academia. The UNIX and NT releases provide comprehensive raster and vector processing capabilities. The PC release is vector only.
ArcView	A commercial desktop mapping/GIS package from ESRI, more user-friendly than ARC/Info.
ASCII	American Standard Code for Information Interchange. A text file format.
BMP	BitMaP. A file extension indicating a graphics file, common in Microsoft Windows applications.
CAD	Computer-Aided Design. The design activities, including drafting and illustrating, in which information processing systems are used to carry out functions such as designing or improving a part or a product.
Contors	A program by John Haigh used to download, process and display archaeological geophysical survey data.
CP/M	CP/M was one of the first true computer operating systems, now superseded by DOS, Windows, and so on.
DBF	A commercial relational database format, initially developed for dbase. Widely used within archaeology.
dGPS	Differential Global Positioning System.
DWF	Digital Web Format. A format for displaying CAD files over the Internet.
DXF	Digital eXchange Format. A format to transfer drawings between Computer-Aided Design systems widely used as an industry standard in the engineering and construction industries.

Earth resistance survey	When passing an electrical current through the ground the measured electrical resistance is indicative of buried features. The configuration of the four necessary electrodes can have many forms and is usually one of the following arrays: twin-probe, Wenner, equidistant double dipole, general double dipole or Schlumberger.
ECEF	Earth-Centred, Earth-Fixed. A cartesian coordinate system used for GPS satellite positioning data.
EDM	Electronic Distance Meter. Electronic distance measuring device used within terrestrial survey. It is based upon the transit time measurement of a light beam emitted from a transmitter to a reflecting target prism and back again. Sometimes incorrectly used to identify Total Station integrated survey instruments, one component of which is an integral EDM.
EH	English Heritage is the national body created in 1984 by Parliament, charged with the protection of the historic environment and with promoting public understanding and enjoyment of it (Online: http://www.english-heritage.org.uk/).
EH GSdb	English Heritage Geophysical Survey Database
Electrostatic survey	Geophysical survey technique that injects electrical currents into the ground through extended flat pads rather than inserted electrodes.
Excel	A commonly used spreadsheet program from Microsoft.
GCP	Ground Control Point
Geoplot	A commercially available program from Geoscan Research used to download, process and display geophysical survey data.
GeoTIFF	An extension to the TIFF graphics standard to incorporate georeferencing information. Although currently supported by a limited number of proprietary GIS, many manufacturers are committed to supporting the standard. It aims to provide a platform-independent method for archiving and transferring spatially referenced raster products.
GPR	Ground Penetrating Radar. Geophysical survey instrument that sends electromagnetic pulses of high frequency (about 500MHz) into the ground and records the delay of their reflection.
GIF	Graphics Interchange Format. A bitmap graphics format from CompuServe which stores computer images in a loss-less compressed format and aims to maintain their correct colours even when transferred between different computers.
GIS	Geographic Information System.
GPS	Global Positioning System.
HTML	Hyper Text Mark-up Language. The general framework for defining document structure used with the World Wide Web facility of the Internet.

InSite	A commercial geophysical survey management and analysis program from GeoQuest.
IFA	The Institute of Field Archaeologists is the professional body for UK archaeologists. The IFA seeks to advance the practice of archaeology through the promotion of professional standards and ethics for the conservation, management and study of the historic environment (Online: http://www.archaeologists.net/).
JPEG	Joint Photographic Expert Group. The original name of the committee that designed this image compression algorithm. The compression leads to an irrecoverable degradation of images based on the substitution of similar colours. This is not noticeable for 'natural', real-world scenes but can have dramatic effects for greyscale images or images with a limited number of colours.
LaTeX	An enhanced version of the free TeX document typesetting software.
Lotus123	A widely used spreadsheet program.
Low frequency electromagnetic survey	A geophysical survey technique based on the transmission and reception of electromagnetic signals of frequencies below 100kHz.
LZW compression	A loss-less image compression algorithm, mainly used with TIFF files.
Magnetometer survey	A geophysical survey technique based on the measurement of local magnetic fields. Buried archaeological features have the potential to affect the measured field. A number of sensor types (e.g. fluxgates, proton free precession, alkaline vapour) can be used and they can be arranged in different ways (e.g. single sensor, gradiometer).
Magnetotelluric survey	A geophysical survey technique that measures variation in magnetic fields caused by currents which are induced in the earth's crust.
Magnetic susceptibility	The ability of a material (e.g. soil) to attain a magnetisation when exposed to a magnetic field.
mda	The mda is a national body that actively ensures that UK museums and heritage bodies are equipped to realise their information assets, to fulfil their educational remit and to demonstrate accountability for their collections.
Metadata	'Data about data'. Information that is used to discover data sets in an archive. Typical metadata are the name of the creator of a resource, a brief description, location of the archive etc.
MGC	The Museums and Galleries Commission is the national advisory body that existed to safeguard and promote UK museums and galleries. The MGC was merged with the Libraries and Information Commission on 1 April 2000 to create the Museums, Libraries and Archives Commission (MLAC).

MIF/MID	Mapinfo export formats.
Microgravity survey	A geophysical survey technique that relies on the accuracy of local gravity constants to derive information on buried features.
NTF	The National Transfer Format. An implementation of British Standard BS7567, used for the transfer of geographic data. It is administered by the Association for Geographic Information in the United Kingdom.
ODA	A document exchange format.
Paradox	A commonly used database package.
PDF	Portable Document Format. A document standard promoted by Adobe.
PNG	Portable Network Graphics. Pronounced 'ping'. The PNG format is intended to provide a portable, legally unencumbered, well-compressed, well-specified standard for loss-less bit-mapped image files. Although the initial motivation for developing PNG was to replace GIF, the design provides some useful new features not available in GIF, with minimal cost to developers (Online: http://www.eps.mcgill.ca/~steeve/PNG/png.html).
Postscript	Postscript is a page description language from Adobe.
Pseudosection	By systematically expanding and moving an earth resistance array some depth profiling can be achieved.
QuattroPro	A spreadsheet software.
Radioactivity survey	By mapping the local radioactivity (either as total counts or as gamma-spectroscopy) information on underlying features may be obtained.
RCAHMS	The Royal Commission on the Ancient and Historical Monuments of Scotland is an independent non-departmental government body financed by Parliament through The Scottish Office under the sponsorship of Historic Scotland (Online: http://www.rcahms.gov.uk/about.html).
RCAHMW	The Royal Commission on the Ancient and Historical Monuments of Wales is an executive non-departmental government body funded through the Welsh Office. The RCAHMW exists to record, interpret and promote a greater appreciation of the Welsh historic environment (Online: http://www.rcahmw.org.uk/)
RTF	Rich Text Format. A widely used document exchange format.
Seismic survey	A geophysical survey technique that is based on the measurement of delay times of acoustic waves injected into the ground.
SDTS	Spatial Data Transfer Standard. A United States Federal standard designed to support the transfer of different types of geographic and cartographic spatial data. This standard specifies a structure and content for spatially referenced data in order to facilitate data transfer between dissimilar spatial database

	systems. Also known as Federal Information Processing Standard (FIPS) 173.
SGML	Standard Generalised Mark-up Language. An ISO Standard defining the general framework for describing a document structure.
SMA	The Society of Museum Archaeologists is committed to the encouragement of museum involvement in field archaeology and the proper curation of the archive.
SMR	Sites and Monuments Record.
TeX	A free document typesetting software.
TIFF	Tagged Interchange File Format. An industry-standard raster image format. TIFF supports black-and-white, grey-scale, pseudocolour, and true-colour images, all of which can be stored in a compressed or uncompressed format. TIFF is commonly used in desktop publishing and serves as an interface to numerous scanners and graphic arts packages.
Tomography	Similar to 'Pseudosection' but with varying electrode arrays and computer controlled.
Total station	A conventional surveying instrument combining an electronic theodolite and an EDM.
Vertical resistivity section	Geophysical technique that indicates the variation of earth resistivity with depth. Is based on the gradual expansion of an electrode array about a centre point.
VLF	Very Low Frequency. A geophysical survey technique based on electromagnetic waves which are transmitted from fixed antennas for air and sea navigation.
WGS 84	The World Geodetic System 1984 is a latitude/longitude earth coordinate system often used for GPS data.
Word	A commonly used word processing package from Microsoft.
Wordperfect	A commonly used word processing package.

Bibliography

Archaeology Data Service. 1998. *Guidelines for Depositors.* Online: http://ads.ahds.ac.uk/project/ userinfo/deposit.html

Archaeology Data Service. 1999. *Collections Policy.* Online: http://ads.ahds.ac.uk/project/ collpol3.html

Archaeology Data Service. 2000. *Charging Policy.* Online: http://ads.ahds.ac.uk/project/userinfo/ charging2.html

Aspinall, A. and Crummett, J.G. 1997. The Electrical Pseudo-section, *Archaeological Prospection*, Vol. 4(1), 37–47

Aspinall, A. and Lynam, J. 1968. Induced polarization as a technique for archaeological surveying, *Prospezioni Archeologiche*, Vol. 3, 91–93

Austin, T., Robinson, D. and Westcott, K. 2001. A Digital Future for our Excavated Past, in Stancic, Z and Veljanovski, 2001 *Computing Applications and Quantative Methods in Archaeology, Proceedings of the 28th Conference, Ljublijana, April 2000*, BAR International Series 931, p 289–296

Beagrie, N. and Greenstein, D. 1998. *A Strategic Framework for Creating and Preserving Digital Resources.* Library Information Technology Centre, South Bank University, London. Online: http:// ahds.ac.uk/manage/framework.htm

Bettess, F. 1992. *Surveying for archaeologists*, 2nd edition, University of Durham, Department of Archaeology, Durham

Cadw and RCAHMW. 1998. *Strategy for Recording and Preserving the Archaeology of Wales*

Clark, A. 1996. *Seeing Beneath the Soil, Prospecting methods in archaeology*, 2nd edition, Batsford, London

Clarke, S. and Robinson, D. forthcoming, '*Geophysical Survey at Leptiminus*' in D.J. Stone, D.J. Mattingly and N. Ben Lazreg (eds), *Leptiminus (Lamta) Report Number 3. The Survey*, Journal of Roman Archaeology Supplementary Series, Portsmouth, Rhode Island

Condron, F., Richards, J., Robinson, D. and Wise, A. 1999. *Strategies for Digital Data – Findings and Recommendations from Digital Data in Archaeology: a Survey of User Needs.* Archaeology Data Service, York

Conyers, L.B. and Goodman, D. 1997. *Ground penetrating radar: an introduction for archaeologists*, AltaMira Press, Walnut Creek, CA

Dodson, A.H. and Haines-Young, R.H.,1993. Datum Transformations and data integration in a GIS environment, pp.79–90 in P.M. Mather (ed.) *Geographical Information Handling – Research and Applications*, John Wiley and Sons Ltd, Chichester

Eder-Hinterleitner, A., Neubauer, W. and Melichar, P. 1996. Restoring Magnetic Anomalies, *Archaeological Prospection*, Vol. 3(4), 185–97

English Heritage. 1991. *Management of Archaeological Projects*, 2nd edition.

English Heritage. 1995. *Geophysical survey in archaeological field evaluation*, Research and Professional Services Guideline No. 1, English Heritage, London

Gaffney, C., Gater, J. and Ovenden, S. 1991. *The Use of Geophysical Techniques in Archaeological Evaluations*, IFA Technical Paper No. 9, IFA

Historic Scotland. 1996a. Historic Scotland Operational Policy Paper #2: *Publication and Archiving of Archaeological Projects*

Historic Scotland. 1996b. *Project Design, Implementation and Archiving*

Kelly, M.A., Dale, P. and Haigh, J.G.B. 1984. A microcomputer system for data logging in geophysical surveying, *Archaeometry*, Vol. 26, 183–91

Linford, P. and Cottrell, P. 1997. *The English Heritage Geophysical Survey Database: Part I: Data Structure and Definitions*, AML Report 72/96, English Heritage, London

Lyons, L. 1991. *A Practical Guide to Data Analysis for Physical Science Students*, Cambridge University Press, Cambridge

Miller, P. and Greenstein, D. 1997. *Discovering Online Resources Across the Humanities: A Practical Implementation of the Dublin Core.* Bath: UKOLN

Museums and Galleries Commission. 1992. *Standards in the Museum Care of Archaeological Collections.* MGC. London

Northamptonshire Heritage. 1998. *Data Standards and Guidance for Digital Data Transfer to the Northamptonshire SMR*, Northamptonshire Heritage

Panissod, G., Dabas, M., Florsch, N., Hesse, A., Jolivet, A., Tabbagh, A. and Tabbagh, J.1998. Archaeological prospecting using electric and electrostatic mobile arrays, *Archaeological Prospection*, Vol. 5(4), 239–51

RCAHMS. 1996. *Guidelines for Archiving of Archaeological Projects.* Royal Commission on the Ancient and Historical Monuments of Scotland. Edinburgh

RCHME. 1995. *Thesaurus of Monument Types*, Royal Commission on the Historical Monuments of England, Swindon

RCHME. 1998. *MIDAS: A Manual and Data Standard for Monument Inventories*, Royal Commission on the Historical Monuments of England, Swindon

Scollar, I., Tabbagh, A., Hesse, A. and Herzog, I. 1990. *Archaeological Prospecting and Remote Sensing*, Cambridge University Press, Cambridge

Society of Museum Archaeologists. 1993. *Selection, Retention and Dispersal of Archaeological Collections: Guidelines for use in England, Wales and Northern Ireland.*

Society of Museum Archaeologists. 1995. *Towards an Accessible Archive. The Transfer of Archaeological Archives to Museums: Guidelines for Use in England, Northern Ireland, Scotland and Wales.*

Stove, G.C. and Addyman, P.V. 1989. Ground Probing Impulse Radar – An Experiment in Archaeological Remote-Sensing at York, *Antiquity*, Vol. 63, 337–42

Swain, H. 1998. *A Survey of Archaeological Archives in England*, English Heritage and Museums & Galleries Commission, London

Walker, R. (ed.) 1993. *AGI Standards Committee GIS Dictionary*, Association for Geographic Information

Wise, A.L. and Miller, P. 1997. Why Metadata Matters in Archaeology. In *Internet Archaeology* 2. Online: http://intarch.ac.uk/journal/issue2/wise_index.html

Appendix 1: Geospatial References

A1.1 LOCATING GEOPHYSICAL RESULTS WITHIN THE WIDER LANDSCAPE

To use geophysical results for other archaeological investigations the location of a survey within the landscape or site must be known. Depending on the intended use, the required accuracy of such information may vary. For example, in order to direct excavations to the areas indicated by geophysical findings a precise reference to the archaeological site grid is required. On the other hand, if only a landscape assessment is required, including aerial photographic interpretations, accuracy is less critical. However, since future demands cannot be predicted, it is essential to record survey positions with the highest possible accuracy in the first place. If existing survey data are to be re-used but spatial information is insufficient, the only solution is to undertake several well-referenced keyhole surveys to relate previous results to accurate site coordinates. This is time consuming and can be avoided through careful documentation in the first place.

This appendix will introduce the concepts of reference frames, their coregistration, georeferencing and issues relating to information accuracy. This discussion is intended to provide a foundation for the recommendations on geospatial project documentation in Section 3.3.

A1.2 REFERENCE FRAMES

In the context of archaeological geophysics, a *reference frame* is a *coordinate system*, based on a *model* of the physical world that allows specification of a spatial position by providing its *coordinates*. The choice of a reference frame depends on the intended use of this positional information, as illustrated below.

A1.2.1 Latitude and longitude

Locations are often specified by providing information on latitude and longitude, with the implicit assumption that the earth can be described as a globe (this is the *model* used) with a coordinate system where 0° longitude is normally assigned to the meridian through Greenwich and 0° latitude to the equator. The *model*, together with this *coordinate system*, is the *reference frame*. The numerical values for longitude and latitude are the *coordinates*. Had the same model been used, but with a different coordinate system (e.g. the 0-meridian running through Rio de Janeiro) different coordinates would need to be used to specify the same point. This illustrates how coordinates are only useful if specified together with their respective reference frame (i.e. the model of the earth and an associated coordinate system).

A1.2.2 Great Britain National Grid

Another common geographic reference frame in Britain is the *Great Britain National Grid*. For this, the Airy Spheroid is used to approximate the earth's surface for the British Isles and a Modified Transverse Mercator projection allows specification of each position in a metrical Cartesian (i.e. rectangular) coordinate system. To avoid negative coordinates a 'false origin' (i.e. one that is SW of the mathematical Modified Transverse Mercator origin) has been chosen to quote the coordinates. This numerical origin (i.e. the coordinates 0E and 0N) lies south-west of the Isles of Scilly. Where a position is specified in Great Britain National Grid coordinates, this *reference frame* is implicitly used. The Ordnance Survey of Great Britain (OS) has developed a system to quote such coordinates conveniently, specifying the relevant 100km x 100km grid square with a two-letter abbreviation, followed by a numerical expression (e.g. a six-figure grid reference for a 100m x 100m grid square) to denote the location in more detail. However, it has to be borne in mind that the copyright for the use of this notation is held by the Ordnance Survey. It is recommended that the 'eastings' and 'northings' (or 'x' and 'y' coordinates) are stated explicitly for a location, measured from the false origin. Information in such format is also simpler to handle by computerised databases. A coordinate in the Great Britain National Grid reference frame, using a generalised notation for the coordinates, could consist of the eastings, followed by the northings and separated with a comma, or both measures provided as separate items (e.g. 423201, 339236).

A1.2.3 Archaeological site grid

For archaeological field projects *site grids* are often established. These reflect the mapping of the actual positions on the ground to their projection on a virtual horizontal plane. Neglecting the curvature of the earth (a reasonable assumption given the size of most archaeological sites), the spatial model used is a flat horizontal projection with a Cartesian coordinate system. Hence the coordinates are specified as 'eastings' and 'northings' within this *reference frame*.

A1.2.4 Geophysics reference frame

The most commonly used *geophysics reference frame* consists of a Cartesian coordinate system on a flat model space. The relationship between this geophysics reference frame and the real world, however, is much more complex than for the site grid. While the latter is simply a projection of the real space onto a horizontal plane, the geophysics frame is determined by the physical layout of grids, often with strings. It is thus warped and stretched over the undulating topographical surface. It is important to remember, however, that despite the resulting distortions in physical space, the geophysics reference frame itself, as a mathematical model, is a perfectly flat and rectangular system. When discussing a geophysics coordinate system one implicitly assumes this reference frame.

A1.3 COREGISTRATION

The choice of a reference frame is often governed by the intended use of the spatial information. A geophysics reference frame, for example, is best suited to represent the geophysical data recorded in a survey. In contrast, the Great Britain National Grid may be the best choice for the mapping of aerial photographic evidence onto Ordnance Survey maps. In many cases, however, the data recorded in one frame have to be used in other frames. The geophysical data may, for example, have to be compared to excavation results recorded on a site grid or with aerial photographs located on the Great Britain National Grid. The task of tying the reference frames together is called *coregistration*.

A1.3.1 Control points

The easiest way of defining a coregistration is to provide a list of points with their respective coordinates in all reference frames concerned. These points are sometimes referred to as control points, reference points, tie points or tics. Often these points are features that can easily be identified in the individual frames. A good example is the rectification of aerial photographs where prominent features (e.g. road crossings or corners of houses) are identified on the photograph and on the map.

To coregister a geophysics frame and a site grid, for example, one could, as a first approximation, provide the coordinates for corners of geophysics 20m x 20m grids (e.g. 0/0; 20/0; 60/100 in the geophysics frame) and their respective coordinates in the site grid (e.g. 0E0N; 18E2N; 56E104N) as measured with, for example, a Total Station. For an undulating topography, many more control points are required to establish the relationship between the frames. Due to the stretching of the geophysics grid over the undulating topography, the coordinates of the geophysics frame will not normally be the same as the coordinates of the site grid. Equipped with a list of common reference points, the mathematical process of transforming a data set from one frame into another can be undertaken. The algorithms used depend on the number of control points provided and whether they should be matched exactly or with a minimisation of errors. Details on various algorithms (e.g. linear, polynomial, spline) may be found, for example, in Scollar *et al.* 1990, p.210.

A1.3.2 Transformation

The explicit specification of the equations for the mathematical transformation between coordinates provides another means of describing a coregistration. The simplest mathematical approach is an *affine transformation*. It consists of stretching (in X and Y direction), rotating (by an angle) and a translation (along X and Y axis). This can therefore be described with 5 parameters (sometimes 6 parameters are provided to allow for a simpler calculation, as with ESRI's software products, like ArcInfo and ArcView). If it is assumed that the stretching in X and Y direction is the same (e.g. on a flat surface), the transformation can be determined from the coordinates of two points alone, otherwise three or more points are required to find the best matching parameter set. It is unusual to specify more complex transformations (e.g. polynomial, spline) explicitly.

A1.4 GEOREFERENCING

Tying reference frames together (coregistration) is sufficient for some applications (e.g. map production) but in many cases a correlation between spatial data and a position on the ground must be established. For example, in order to use geophysical evidence to direct the location of an excavation trench, the actual position of the geophysical anomaly *on the ground* has to be known. Relating spatial data to actual ground positions is termed *georeferencing* (note that the term is used by some authors to include coregistration).

Georeferencing is best undertaken by relating the reference frame concerned to features on the ground (Ground Control Points, GCPs) that are reasonably permanent (e.g. the concrete bases of a pylon). It is also advantageous to select features that can be identified on maps in order to provide information for later coregistration (see A.1.3). If no such features exist, the only solution may be to introduce man-made markers that can, hopefully, be found again in the future. Such markers may be wooden or plastic pegs of reasonable dimensions that are either driven deeply into the ground or set in concrete. Clearly, if such man-made markers are used, permission has to be sought and the design must minimise any risk to people or animals.

Once GCPs have been selected and very carefully documented (e.g. which corner of a pylon's base, or which side of a wall) their relationship to the reference frame has to be recorded. The method used will depend on the nature of the reference frame and the methods available to establish it.

If, for example, a site grid was set out with a Total Station and if it will most likely be re-established with such an instrument, georeferencing information may simply comprise the site grid coordinates for two GCPs together with details on the accuracy of the recording. Later measurements of the two GCPs with a Total Station from any point on the site will allow determination of the position and orientation of the Total Station and hence the site grid. In order to secure a uniform level of accuracy, it is advantageous if the two GCPs are spaced at the opposite sides of the area to be surveyed.

In contrast, if a reference frame has been laid out on the ground from baselines (e.g. a geophysics grids system, see Section 3.3.1), their most relevant points (e.g. ends and intersections) should be measured from the GCPs, for example with tapes. For each selected point, measurements from at least two GCPs must be taken. The record of these measurements, together with estimated accuracies, will allow later relocation of the baselines.

A1.5 ABSOLUTE COORDINATES USING GPS

The Global Positioning System (GPS) consists of a network of satellites which continuously transmit information that can be converted by a ground-based receiver into its own absolute coordinates on the earth's surface. No reference to maps or GCPs is required. The details of GPS are explained by Walker (1993) and this concept is an ideal solution to many applications which require positional information. However, there are several factors that influence the possible use of GPS for surveying.

Most importantly, the accuracy of positional information for a basic device is only about 3m to 10m due to inherent features of the system. If, however a differential GPS (dGPS) is employed, accuracies of better than 1cm can be achieved. For dGPS to work, a permanent GPS base station has to be set up at a fixed location that provides the mobile receiver with relative locational data, either in real time or with post-processing software. A convenient solution is the use of commercial GPS base stations that transmit their correction signal on FM frequencies ('beacons'). Such real time differential GPS can achieve lateral accuracies of about 1m. While lateral accuracy can be improved by observing several satellites simultaneously, information on vertical positions can only be derived from satellites above the receiver. Therefore, the vertical accuracy of dGPS systems is only about half the lateral accuracy.

GPS systems measure the relative positions of receiver and satellites using an 'Earth-Centred, Earth-Fixed' Cartesian coordinate system (ECEF). This system, which is aligned with the World Geodetic System 1984 (WGS 84) reference ellipsoid, has its origin close to the earth's centre of mass, its z axis parallel to the axis of rotation of the earth and its x axis passing through the intersection of the equator and the Greenwich meridian. Fortunately most receivers convert ECEF coordinates to WGS 84 latitude, longitude and height for output, and some will also perform transformations to other datums and coordinate systems, for example to the Great Britain National Grid. However, it has to be remembered that for historic reasons the Great Britain National Grid is not homogeneous and, despite complex conversion algorithms, differences between map- and GPS-derived National Grid coordinates can be up to 2m (Dodson and Haines-Young 1993).

A1.6 PRECISION, RESOLUTION AND ACCURACY

It is worthwhile considering how coordinates are specified in different reference frames. In this respect the terms precision, resolution and accuracy need to be explained.

A1.6.1 Precision

Precision of a coordinate (or indeed of any variable) is determined by the numerical format used to represent it. If, for example, a metric coordinate is only represented by integer numbers (i.e. without decimal places), its precision is 1m; if an angular measurement is only specified as degrees and minutes its precision is 1 minute; if a map position is specified with a letters-cum-six-figure Great Britain National Grid reference (see above) the precision of this representation is 100m x 100m.

A1.6.2 Resolution

While the precision is only limited by the *numerical format* used, the resolution of a coordinate is determined by its *physical* limitation. For a geophysical survey the closest spacing between adjacent survey lines may, for example, be 0.5m. In this case the spatial resolution of the survey is 0.5m — even if it were recorded with two decimal places (i.e. a precision of 0.01m). On a printed map the shortest distance between distinguishable objects may be 0.5mm; this is the map's resolution and using its scale this can be converted into the ground resolution. For example, a map with a scale of 1:25,000 and a resolution of 0.5mm has a ground resolution of 12.5m. In summary, the resolution is a measure of the smallest separation between distinguishable features.

A1.6.3 Accuracy

Precision and resolution determine the minimal numerical and physical separation of objects in a reference frame. The *accuracy* of a coordinate describes the confidence one can have in finding the object at the given position. This is often referred to as the measurement error.

In order to understand the difference between accuracy and precision a few more comments are appropriate. A typical example for specifying the accuracy of a measurement could be 'the distance to the object is about 20.4m, plus or minus 0.1m'. In this example, the measurement value is 20.4m and its accuracy is 0.1m, which means that the *true* distance could be between 20.3m and 20.5m (for the statistical definition of accuracy as the standard deviation of a statistical error, see, for example, Lyons 1991. If one decided, after this initial measurement, to archive the data in a numerical format that only has a precision of 1m (i.e. the measurement would be represented as 20m) the accuracy would have been reduced to 1m since all measurements between 19.5m and 20.4m would be recorded as the same value. On the other hand, if one used a precision of 0.01m for recording (i.e. the measurement would be represented as 20.40m) the accuracy of the measurement would still not improve beyond 10cm. In conclusion, the accuracy of a measurement can never be better than the precision of the data format, although it can be worse.

A1.6.4 Accuracy and coregistration

It is important to consider what happens to the accuracy of measurements during coregistration. It is the combination of accuracies of the original measurements and of the coregistration process that will determine the accuracy of the final data set, as the following discussion shows.

A geophysical survey may be undertaken along a grid system laid out on the ground. With a careful operator the spatial accuracy for locating a measurement point can be 0.05m. The geophysical data are recorded with this accuracy within their reference frame. In order to tie them to an existing site grid some control points may be measured with a Total Station (see Section 3.3.4). The accuracy of such measurements can be 0.005m. Coregistration of the geophysical data to the site grid will eliminate most of the spatial distortions but will not improve the initial accuracy of 0.05m. For referencing on a smaller scale it may be necessary to relate the site grid to map coordinates in a known coordinate system. In most cases the coregistration between the site grid and the map frame will be based on points measured on a map (paper or digital), the accuracy of the latter being often limited and rarely better than 1m. Hence, expressing all geophysical measurements in coordinates of the map's reference frame (from geophysics, to site, to map) would result in an unnecessarily poor overall accuracy of the geophysical data of about 1m. It is worth remembering that the use of coordinates derived from maps is also covered by copyright.

This example demonstrates that the best approach to providing spatial data is to describe individual reference frames, their internal accuracy and how they relate to each other (providing coregistration information with accuracy details) rather than expressing all data in the most common frame which usually has the worst accuracy. There is one exception to this recommendation. If spatial measurements are made absolutely and with high accuracy (as can be achieved with modern dGPS), no further conversion of reference frames may be required.

A1.6.5 The need for information on accuracy

It has been explained that precision is related to the data format used (e.g. six-figure grid reference) but information on accuracy has to be specified explicitly. This is necessary to assess the usefulness of a data set for a specific purpose. For example, a trial excavation may be undertaken on the basis of a previous geophysical survey. In order to minimise the size of the excavation trench the location of the geophysical anomalies must be provided to a certain accuracy, say 0.5m. Only if it is known that the accuracy of geophysical data within the site grid is of a comparable magnitude can such a 'surgical' excavation trench be established. Otherwise, a much larger area has to be opened 'to be on the safe side'.

Appendix 2: Documentation Overview

A2.1 INTRODUCTION

As discussed throughout this *Guide*, in order to support later re-use it is necessary to record information during the project in addition to capturing raw geophysical survey data. The information recommended for documenting geophysical surveys is described in Sections 2 and 3 of this *Guide*. This appendix is intended to summarise the information recommended and set it in the context in which it will be used. Firstly, the metadata requested by the ADS for ArcHSearch and by English Heritage for their Geophysical Survey database, referred to in Section 5, are described. Finally a check list of all the information recommended in this *Guide* is provided to assist project managers in preparing project documentation.

A2.2 CORE METADATA FOR THE ADS

The metadata requested by the ADS for digital archiving, listed below, is based on Dublin Core Metadata and is used for resource recovery through ArcHSearch, the online catalogue of the ADS (See Section 5.2.1).

Resource discovery metadata is the index level information that is used by gateways through which users seek archival material. 'Metadata', put simply, is data which describes the original information. The Archaeology Data Service, along with a growing number of organisations around the world, advocates the use of the *Dublin Core* metadata set. This comprises a series of fifteen broad categories or elements, each of which is *optional* or may be *repeated* as many times as required. The elements may also be *refined* through the use of a developing set of sub-elements. The use of the Dublin Core within the Archaeology Data Service is discussed further elsewhere (Miller and Greenstein 1997, Wise and Miller 1997), and the current element definitions laid down across the Dublin Core community are available on the Internet.

In addition to the resource discovery metadata described above, the Archaeology Data Service also requests that full documentation accompanies the digital files being deposited. This should include: a list of all file names, explanation of any codes used in the file names, a description of file formats, a list of any codes used in the data, a description of the hardware, software and operating system used for creating the files and the date when the data were last modified.

Information type	Scope note
Survey name	The name of the site, project or survey.
Survey index	The identification number/code used internally for the survey event and the related data.
Survey purpose	A brief summary (max. 200–300 words) of the main aims and objectives of the project from which the data collection arose and the purpose of the geophysical survey.
Survey keywords	Keywords indexing the subject content of the data set. They can be drawn from the data fields listed in Section 3 (e.g. *Solid/Drift geology, Monument type, Survey type* etc.). If a local documentation standard is used this should be included with the data set.
Spatial coverage	The map coordinates of the SW and NE corner of a bounding box enclosing the survey area. For Britain National Grid coordinates are recommended.
Administrative area	The District/County/Unitary Authority in which the survey area lies.
Country	The country in which the survey was undertaken.
Duration	The dates of the first and last day on which the fieldwork took place.
Monument period	The archaeological period(s) of any archaeological monument that is known to exist at the site or that was revealed during the survey.
Depositor	The name, address and role of the organisation or individual(s) who deposited the data related to the geophysical survey.
Related archives	References to the original material for data that were derived in whole or in part from published or unpublished sources, whether printed or machine-readable.
Copyright	A description of any known copyrights held on the source material.

Table 9: ADS Core metadata for geophysical surveys

A2.3 METADATA FOR THE ENGLISH HERITAGE GEOPHYSICAL SURVEY DATABASE

English Heritage requests the same resource discovery metadata as the Archaeology Data Service (see Table 9). However, English Heritage also requests additional descriptive metadata for geophysical surveys recorded in its Geophysical Survey Database (see Section 5.2.2). The additional metadata requested are listed in Table 10.

Information type	Scope note
Bibliographic references	Relevant bibliographic information about the site or project.
Solid geology	The underlying solid geology.
Drift geology	Relevant drift geology for the survey area.
Weather	A brief description of weather during fieldwork, with clear reference to previous conditions.
Land use	The land use at the time of the survey.
Monument type	A classification of any archaeological monument that is known to exist at the site or that was revealed during the survey.
Scheduled Ancient Monument (SAM) number	Any sites within the survey area which have been included on the Schedule of Ancient Monuments should be identified by their county SAM number.
Surveyor	The name and address of the organisation or individual(s) who carried out the geophysical survey.
Client	The name and address of the organisation or individual(s) who commissioned the survey.
Primary archive	The name and address of the organisation or individual(s) holding the primary data from the survey.
Survey type	The generic category of geophysical technique used.
Instrumentation	Specific information about the type and configuration of the geophysical instruments used.
Area surveyed	The area of ground covered with each survey technique.

Method of coverage	The method by which the ground was covered and the data were acquired.
Traverse separation	The separation (or distance) between adjacent lines.
Reading interval	If data were recorded at regular intervals along the traverses, the distance in metres between adjacent readings should be noted.
Additional remarks (for data collection)	It is also important to note any other technical aspects of the survey which may have a bearing.
Probe configuration	Earth resistance electrode configuration used.
Probe spacing	The distance between adjacent electrodes.
Report title	The title of the initial paper or digital report that has been generated from the results of the survey.
Report reference number	Surveyor's reference number.
Report author	The author(s) of the report.
Report holder	The name and address of the organisation(s) or individual(s) from whom copies of the report, or data, may be requested.
Report summary	A brief description of the findings of the survey.

Table 10: Additional metadata elements necessary for the EH GSdb

English Heritage requests that standard terminology lists are used when providing information for inclusion in its Geophysical Survey Database. These lists include: County codes, Monument Period (terms listed in the Manual of Data Standards for Monument Inventories: MIDAS is recommended (RCHME 1998)), Land Use, Solid Geology and Drift Geology (lists are taken from Linford and Cottrell (1997)).

A2.4 A CHECK-LIST FOR DOCUMENTING GEOPHYSICAL SURVEYS

This section offers a check-list of all the information recommended in this *Guide* indexed against the metadata requested by the ADS and EH GSdb. This is intended to assist project managers in compiling a summary of the project documentation that should be provided with a geophysical survey archive.

Geophysical survey documentation checklist			
Project description (Section 3.2)	**For ADS**	**For EH GSdb**	**Additional documentation**
Survey name	Y	Y	
Survey index	Y	Y	
Survey purpose (Section 2.3) • Field evaluation in advance of development • Site management • Archaeological research • Technical research	Y	Y	
Bibliographic references		Y	
Survey keywords (Section 3 and Appendix 3)	Y	Y	
Duration	Y	Y	
Location of survey (Section 3.2)	**For ADS**	**For EH GSdb**	**Additional documentation**
Spatial coverage	Y	Y	
Administrative area	Y	Y	
Country	Y	Y	
Local conditions (Section 3.2)	**For ADS**	**For EH GSdb**	**Additional documentation**
Solid geology		Y	
Drift geology		Y	
Weather		Y	
Soil condition			Y
Land use		Y	

Table 11: A documentation checklist (continued over the next 4 pages)

Archaeology	For ADS	For EH GSdb	Additional documentation
Monument type		Y	
Monument period	Y	Y	
Scheduled Ancient Monument (SAM) number		Y	
Roles and repositories (Section 3.2)	For ADS	For EH GSdb	Additional documentation
Surveyor		Y	
Client		Y	
Depositor	Y	Y	
Primary archive		Y	
Related archives	Y	Y	
Copyright	Y	Y	
Reasons for choice of survey methods and procedure (Section 2.4)	For ADS	For EH GSdb	Additional documentation
Survey objectives			Y
Archaeological questions			Y
Previous aerial photographic evidence			Y
Previous geophysical survey results			Y
Current land use			Y
Previous land use			Y
Underlying solid and drift geology			Y
Other local geomorphological and topographic factors			Y
Degree of access to land			Y
Time, money and personnel available for the survey			Y

Geophysics coordinate system (Section 3.3.1)	For ADS	For EH GSdb	Additional documentation
Procedure used to lay out the grid			Y
Estimates of accuracies for re-establishing the grid			Y
Georeferencing (Section 3.3.1)	For ADS	For EH GSdb	Additional documentation
Description and approximate location of ground features for reference			Y
Distance to ground features for key points along the baseline			Y
Compass bearing of baseline			Y
Coregistration with site grid (Section 3.3.2)	For ADS	For EH GSdb	Additional documentation
Coordinates of control points, both in the geophysics coordinate system and the site grid (with accuracies)			Y
Site coordinates of map-features, if coregistration with maps is required			Y
Site coordinates of ground features used for georeferencing			Y
Data collection	For ADS	For EH GSdb	Additional documentation
Data collection for all survey types (Section 3.4)			
Survey type		Y	
Instrumentation		Y	

Area surveyed		Y	
Method of coverage		Y	
Traverse separation		Y	
Reading interval		Y	
Sampling position			Y
Grid size			Y
Accuracies (spatial and of readings)			Y
Additional remarks (for data collection)		Y	
Data collection for earth resistance surveys (Section 3.4)			
Probe configuration		Y	
Probe spacing		Y	
Data collection for magnetometer surveys (Section 3.4)			
Direction of Magnetic North			Y
Whether instrument drift was recorded			Y
Data collection for GPR surveys (Section 3.4)			
Timing			Y
Dielectric permittivity			Y
Documenting the grids (Section 3.5)	**For ADS**	**For EH GSdb**	**Additional documentation**
Grid layout and list of grid names			Y
Grid size			Y
Resolution			Y
Survey direction			Y
Line sequence			Y

	For ADS	For EH GSdb	Additional documentation
Drift value			Y
Bias value			Y
Dummy value			Y
Overrange value			Y
Documenting data treatment (Section 3.6)	For ADS	For EH GSdb	Additional documentation
Processing steps			Y
Images and reports (Sections 3.8 and 3.9)	For ADS	For EH GSdb	Additional documentation
Figure caption (separately for each image)			Y
Report title		Y	
Report reference number		Y	
Report author		Y	
Report holder		Y	
Report summary		Y	
Documentation about the digital files	For ADS	For EH GSdb	Additional documentation
List of all file names	Y		
Explanation of codes used in file names	Y		
Description of file formats	Y		
List of codes used in files	Y		
Hardware, software and operating system used for creation	Y		
Date of last modification	Y		
Description of known errors in data			Y
Indications of known areas of weakness in data			Y

Appendix 3: Standards

CONTENT STANDARDS

FISH – The Forum on Information Standards in Heritage
FISH exists to promote and develop standards covering the compilation and organisation of archaeological and architectural heritage 'inventories' (online: http://www.mda.org.uk/FISH/). The work of FISH has two complimentary starting points, MIDAS (online: http://www.rchme.gov.uk/midas/index.html) and INSCRIPTION. Of these two standards, INSCRIPTION has more relevance for the archaeological geophysicist.

Inscription – Inscription provides a set of word lists to describe the built and buried heritage (online: http://www.mda.org.uk/fish/inscript.htm). It is hoped that the Inscription standard will provide a useful starting point for the establishment of common UK-wide terminology standards. Inscription provides the wordlists in a format suitable for inclusion into a range of modern databases. It is recommended that INSCRIPTION approved terms are utilised in the documentation of geophysical surveys, for example, Monument Types should be drawn from either the English Thesaurus of Monument Types or the forthcoming Scottish Thesaurus of Monument Types, where appropriate.

The wordlists are organised by MIDAS units of information and include:

- Archaeological archive types
- English civil parishes
- REP93 Condition
- RCHME Thesaurus of building materials
- English County list
- Currency
- Date range qualifier
- English district areas
- ALGAO Event types (surveys)
- Event types (interpretation)
- ALGAO Event types (interventions)
- Evidence thesaurus
- Internal cross reference qualifiers
- REP93 Land use
- ALGAO Consultation Outcome list
- ALGAO Consultation type
- ALGAO Work proposed
- Defence of Britain Thesaurus

- Thesaurus of Monument Types
- Co-ordinate set precision
- English non-parish areas
- RCHME Archaeological Periods list
- REP93 Topology
- English Unitary authorities

In addition to the standards included in the INSCRIPTION word lists, there are a number of other important content standards that have relevance to the archaeological geophysicist.

Solid and Drift Geology – The terms included in these lists are drawn from English Heritage's Geophysical Survey Database and are based on the 1:625000 Geological Map of the United Kingdom (Solid Geology) 3rd Edition, 1979 (Online: http://ads.ahds.ac.uk/project/userinfo/geology.html). The British Geological Survey Lexicon of Named Rock Units should be consulted for a complete up to date list of terms for solid and drift geology (Online: http://www.bgs.ac.uk/lexicon/lexicon_intro.html).

National Geospatial Data Framework – This important co–operative initiative is aiming to provide effective means of access to geospatial data collected and held by government and the public and private sectors following a model potentially similar to that of the AHDS. NGDF is addressing issues such as metadata standardisation and is looking to greatly increase the market for existing and new data (Online: http://www.ngdf.org.uk/).

PROFESSIONAL STANDARDS

Institute of Field Archaeologists (IFA) – The IFA is the professional organisation for UK archaeologists (Online: http://www.archaeologists.net). It promotes professional standards and ethics for conserving, managing, understanding and promoting enjoyment of the heritage. The IFA has constitutional Codes of Conduct and Bylaws for:
- Area and special interest groups
- By-laws amplifying Articles 9–11 and defining 'competence'
- Code of approved practice for the regulation of contractual arrangements in field archaeology
- Code of conduct
- Disciplinary regulations
- Regulations for the Registration of archaeological organisations

The IFA is also concerned with setting standards in archaeology. To date it has standards documents pertaining to:
- Desk-based assessment
- Field evaluation
- Watching brief
- Excavation
- Building investigation and recording
- Finds

The standards documents have several useful appendices that document items to cover in:

- Project specification
- Project design
- Post-excavation project design

Management of Archaeological Projects (MAP2) – This standard document was developed by English Heritage as a guide to the management of all phases of archaeological projects. MAP2 includes guidelines for planning, fieldwork, assessment of potential, analysis, report preparation, and archiving (Online: http://www.eng-h.gov.uk/guidance/map2/).

ARCHIVAL AND OTHER USEFUL STANDARDS

Digital Archives from Excavation and Fieldwork: *A Guide to Good Practice*. The primary aim of this Digital Archiving Guide to Good Practice is to provide information on the best way to create and document digital material produced in the course of excavation and fieldwork, and to deposit it safely in a digital archive facility for future use. It was written by the ADS with contributions from a wide range of authors (Online: http://ads/ahds.ac.uk/project/goodguides/excavation/).

Elib Standards Guidelines (Version 2) – This covers, concisely, a wide range of electronic format and interchange standards, and includes references to more detailed reading (Online: http://www.ukoln.ac.uk/services/elib/papers/other/standards).

JISC/TLTP Copyright Guidelines – This document is targeted at the HE audience and covers a wide range of copyright issues in electronic media (Online: http://www.ukoln.ac.uk/services/elib/papers/other/jisc-tltp/jisc.pdf).

Towards an Accessible Archaeological Archive. The Transfer of Archaeological Archives to Museums: Guidelines for Use in England, Northern Ireland, Scotland and Wales – The Society of Museum Archaeologists 1995 guide, edited by Janet Owen, provides detailed information about all aspects of preparing an archive for deposit in a museum. It does not cover digital archiving explicitly, but does provide detailed advice on documentary archives with sources of information and a bibliography.

International Core Data Standard for Archaeological Sites and Monuments (Draft) – Produced by CIDOC, the International Documentation Committee of the International Council of Museums, this document guides the user in documenting archaeological sites and monuments. The goal of this standard is to facilitate international exchange of information by encouraging standardised approaches to database structure (Online: http://www.natmus.min.dk/cidoc/archsite/coredata/arch1.htm).

Informing the Future of the Past: *Guidelines for SMRs*. This aims to provide an introduction to managing, creating and using sites and monuments records. The guidelines are based on nationally agreed standards and the experiences of working SMR Officers. Edited by Kate Fernie and Paul Gilman and published by English Heritage in 2000.

For more information on the most relevant archaeological standards see:
http://ads.ahds.ac.uk/project/userinfo/standards.html